The Best
Women's Stage Monologues
of 1995

Other books by Jocelyn A. Beard

100 Men's Stage Monologues from the 1980's
100 Women's Stage Monologues from the 1980's
The Best Men's/Women's Stage Monologues of 1990
The Best Men's/Women's Stage Monologues of 1991
The Best Men's/Women's Stage Monologues of 1992
The Best Men's/Women's Stage Monologues of 1993
The Best Men's/Women's Stage Monologues of 1994

ologues of 1994
m the 1980's
rom the 1980's
1992
1993

The Best Stage Scenes of 1994
The Best Stage Scenes of 1995
Monologues from Classic Plays 468 B.C. to 1960 A.D.
Scenes from Classic Plays 468 B.C. to 1970 A.D.
100 Great Monologues from the Renaissance Theatre
100 Great Monologues from the Neo-Classical Theatre
100 Great Monologues from the 19th C. Romantic & Realistic Theatre

The Best
Women's Stage Monologues
of 1995

edited by Jocelyn A. Beard

The Monologue Audition Series

SK
A Smith and Kraus Book

Published by Smith and Kraus, Inc.
One Main Street, Lyme, NH 03768

First Edition: March 1996
10 9 8 7 6 5 4 3 2 1

The Monologue Audition Series ISSN 1067-134X

NOTE: These monologues are intended to be used for audition and class study; permission is not required to use the material for those purposes. However, if there is a paid performance of any of the monologues included in this book, please refer to the permissions acknowledgment pages to locate the source who can grant permission for public performance.

Contents

Preface, Jocelyn A. Beard vii

Introduction, Susan Gregg ix

Amnesia, Robert Anasi 1

Blink of an Eye, Jeremy Dobrish 2

bliss, Benjamin Bettenbender 3

By the Sea: Dusk Terrence McNally 5

A Candle in the Window, Tom Gilroy 6

A Cheever Evening, A.R. Gurney *(2)* 7

Collateral Damage, Mansel Robinson *(2)* 9

Company Policy, Michael Ajakwe Jr. *(2)* 12

Crow, Louis Nowra 16

Dates and Nuts, Gary Lennon *(2)* 18

A Dead Man's Apartment, Edward Allan Baker 22

Demons, Robert Brustein 23

Dog Opera, Constance Congdon *(2)* 25

Down By The Ocean, P.J. Barry 28

Drive Like Jackson Pollock, Steven Tanenbaum 30

THE EIGHT: Reindeer Monologues, Jeff Goode 31

Emma's Child, Kristine Thatcher *(3)* 34

Emotions, Robert Coles 38

Gunplay, Frank Higgins 39

Half-Court, Brian Silberman 41

If We Are Women, Joanna McClelland Glass 42

Jaws of Life, Jocelyn Beard *(2)* *43*

Lady-Like, Laura Shamas *(2)* *47*

Living in Paradise, Jack Gilhooley 49

Love Knots, Vivienne Plumb *(2)* *53*

Middle-Aged White Guys, Jane Martin 55

The Monogamist, Christopher Kyle 56

The Most Massive Woman Wins, Madeleine George 57

My Darling Gremlin, Greg Tate 59

My Virginia, Darci Picoult 60

New England, Richard Nelson 61

Our Own Marguerite, Robert Vivian 62

The Psychic Life of Savages, Amy Freed *(2)* *63*

The Queen's Knight, Frank Cossa *(2)* *65*

Saucy Jack, Sharon Pollock 67

Self-Defense, Michael P. Scasserra 69

Sophistry, Jonathan Marc Sherman 74

Talk/Show, Michael P. Scasserra 75

Tough Choices For the New Century, Jane Anderson 78

Twelve Dreams, James Lapine 79

Watbanaland, Doug Wright 81

Your Obituary Is A Dance, Benard Cummings 82

Permission Acknowledgments 83

Preface

If I had to select one word or concept which I felt best described the 1995 theatrical season it would have to be "struggle." This season has produced numerous interesting roles for women which reflect the various global and domestic upheavals which are currently defining this era. In Constance Congdon's *Dog Opera,* we are introduced to a woman's struggle to reconcile her love for a man with whom she is sexually incompatible. Vivienne Plumb's *Love Knots* tells a poignant story of estranged sisters who struggle to cope with the death of their mother. Madeleine George's *The Most Massive Woman Wins,* illustrates the struggle facing women who fall victim to the demands of body image. And in Michael Ajakwe's *Company Policy,* we meet women struggling against the double threat of racism and sexism.

Struggle and conflict are no strangers to women, and the playwrights of 1995 have given remarkable voice to the process of conflict. This is essential to the continued evolution of theatre. 1995 has proved to be a theatrical watershed in what has so far been a very wild ride.

Please, read these plays for they are important works.

Break a leg!

Jocelyn Beard
Patterson, NY
Winter 1996

To Sharon Fallon at Love Creek Productions with thanks and love for taking me to Vladivostok.

Introduction

It has become customary for both theatre organizations and casting directors to hold general auditions before calling actors in for specific roles. Usually you will be expected to present two contrasting monologues, one from a classic, the other from a contemporary play. The classics are the classics and the selection is finite. The supply of contemporary monologues, however, is replenished almost daily it seems, and the actor who gets the work is the one who continues working on his craft. Among other things, this means continually adding monologues to your repertoire. Selecting monologues for audition purposes is a daunting process but there are actually only two major criterion to consider: what "they" need and what you need. If your selections don't meet both criterion, reconsider your material.

What "they" (the people on the other side of the table in the audition room) need is to get to know you through your work. They need a sense of the idiosyncratic corners of your mind, your sense of humor, your taste in dramatic literature, your understanding of humanity. They want to see inside your soul. Technically, they need to know what your emotional range is, what your voice and body can do, how you handle language, how skillful your text analysis is. They need to get to know you through your work.

You need monologues that allow you to enjoy auditioning. If a monologue doesn't somewhat exceed your reach, it probably isn't challenging enough to keep you interested and if you're not interested, neither are they. If it shows only you and not a character, it will be worthless to you and it won't get you a job. You need monologues which engage and excite you so much you can hardly wait to perform them. Nothing is as exhilarating as watching an actor enjoy acting.

So what are the elements of a good audition monologue?

The text itself must be substantial. It needs to work just like a good play; it needs to transport the actor and the audience from here and now into another realm. It should be about something; just telling a story is usually not enough unless the character has a significant point to make within the body of a monologue. The cuttings from Sharon Pollock's *Saucy Jack* is a good example of a story with a point.

The character needs to be distant enough from you that you have to change yourself in order to fulfill the demands of the character, the monologue and the play. (This means you have to read the whole play. If you don't, inevitably you will be asked questions you can't answer.) Both of the Frank Cossa pieces are likely candidates as the character of Marie Antoinette was not only real and will require a somewhat historically accurate portrayal but she is also layered and complex.

It has to have an arc; something has to have changed from the first word to the last. Madeline, in Congdon's *Dog Opera*, changes during the course of the speech. So does Bernice in the same play.

It has to be different from your other monologue. This means that not only are the characters very different, the general tone, style and form are different. One could be from a Shakespearean tragedy, the other from a Gurney comedy. Clearly the two characters would not be alike and would require different facets of your idiosyncratic self.

It needs to be fresh for your audience. This is perhaps your worst problem. Consider what "they" must be seeing over the course of auditions and make sure you don't show them the tenth Lady Macbeth of the day.

On the other hand, your Medea monologue will probably not help the auditioner know if you might be right for *The Man Who Came To Dinner*. Make it your business to find out what specific plays the theatre is producing if you're doing a general audition for a season, or who the casting director's clients are and what they will be producing.

You can see immediately that you are going to need scores of monologues if you're serious about acting. This book is only one on what will eventually occupy a whole bookshelf in your library. If you don't find one now that strikes your fancy, look again in a few years; you'll be surprised how much you've learned about yourself and how much more you understand about humanity.

We all agree that our way of hiring actors is barbaric at best. You are required to bare your soul on the one hand, yet accept rejection as a matter of course on the other. Rest assured that those of us on the other side of the table find this process as odious as you do. But you should also know that our hopes and expectations rise every time a new actor enters the room. We truly want you to be the delightful discovery of the day, to engage and entertain us. You may not have control of the plays we do or how we do them, but you do have control of how we perceive you in the audition. Part of out perception will rely on what material you choose.

Susan Gregg, Associate Artistic Director, The Repertory Theatre of St. Louis

Amnesia
Robert Anasi

AMELIA: a famous lost aviator, 30-40
SCENE: A laboratory

Here, Amelia describes her obsession with flight.

○   ○   ○

AMELIA: Flying was my obsession. I spent hundreds of hours locked in a Link Blind-Flying Trainer in a hangar in Oakland, until I could have flown under the Golden Gate Bridge with my eyes shut. Every year a little farther, every year a little faster, faster and further, across the Atlantic, across the Pacific, Dakar, London, Brussels, joining cities like jewels on a string. I flew in a tunnel with a drunkard beside me, I took every precaution, my eyes closed. The Cross of the Legion of Honor, National Geographic's gold medal, radio broadcasts, speaking tours. I liked the freedom the money brought me, it meant I could be in the air, moving toward something. I was the golden girl. On my flight to Mexico City the Sonora Desert was as barren from the air as I imagine the surface of the moon to be, the dry, broken ground, and great piles of rock. I felt like I'd stepped off the surface of the world I knew, flown off the edge of the map. I was exhilarated, I understood then, it's why I went in the first place. Millions of people left behind and I was free to go, I could land anywhere there was a level piece of ground fifty yards long. Every landing was a risk, every take-off too. I flew back and forth across America and back and forth. Sometimes in the West the only way I could discover my location was by flying low enough over isolated railroad stations to read their names. I flew over the Grand Canyon at dawn, I saw gigantic herds of cattle raising dust clouds miles wide, I saw the snaking trails of the great American rivers, Missouri, Mississippi, Colorado. With every flight I made the country changed underneath me, the home I returned to wasn't the home I had left. I didn't have a home. I was pushing forty and I'd never been in love, such a small thing. Nothing. And then this came along. To circumnavigate the globe at the equator, it was the last important record, it was to be my last flight.

Blink of an Eye
Jeremy Dobrish

CELESTE: a guardian angel, 20s
SCENE: New York City

Here an angelic visitor begs forgiveness from one of her charges.

○   ○   ○

CELESTE: Well, you see, being a Guardian Angel is not the greatest job you could ever ask for. I mean, yes, you get certain perks. Stopping time's not bad, free fries, whatever, but basically it's a pretty low self-esteem kind of a deal. No matter how hard you try, you're destined to fail right? I mean I can watch and watch and watch, and be your guardian and help out as best I can. But ultimately, one of these days (and I'm not saying it's coming any- time soon OK? so don't get all freaky and weird on me) but one of these days someone or something's gonna act too quickly for me to react and you're gonna get yours.

[BOSWELL: I am?]

CELESTE: I mean it's not like you're my only client you know what I'm saying? I've got a lot of people to look out for. Not to mention the animals, although I must admit the cats are a little easier cause at least I can blow it a few times with them so I don't really watch my cats too closely. Oh, but don't get me wrong…, I like cats. People…, they try to be in the past, present and future all at the same time, while cats live only in the present, in the eternity of an instant. Ever notice that?

bliss
Benjamin Bettenbender

JO-LYNNE: a woman desperately seeking to avenge her husband's death, 30s
SCENE: Here and now

A dispute between neighbors ends in bloodshed, and the grieving Jo-Lynne becomes obsessed with finding someone to kill the man who killed her husband. She finally approaches Chick, a man that she knew years before, and offers him money to execute her neighbor. When Chick refuses, Jo-Lynne reminds him of something that he once said that left her with the impression that he could easily take a life.

JO-LYNNE: She kept saying you would never do it for real, but you said she was wrong. That for you it was like an equation. You had this thing they did to you on one side, and you had maybe going to prison on the other, and if someone did something bad enough to you, so bad that it was worth taking the risk of getting caught, you would do it in a second. *(Pause.)* You remember that?

[CHICK: Can't say as I do, exactly. *(Pause.)* Sounds like me.]

JO-LYNNE: Well I remember it because I thought it was so stupid, you know? Like you were saying getting caught was the only reason not to kill someone. Estrella and I even talked about it afterwards and she said she thought you were just talking shit but I didn't, I thought you meant it. So when we heard about you getting sent to Rahway, I figured that's what it was about. *(Pause.)* When I saw you a few weeks ago working here…it popped into my head again. I thought…I mean, I think…now…that I know what you meant about something being bad enough. That someone could do something so…terrible that just knowing he was alive could be the worst fate you could imagine. That his not being dead could scare you more than anything the police or anyone else could do to you. So killing someone like that…it would be easy. Like you said, it would be like an equation that just worked out. *(Pause.)* Is that what you were talking about?

[CHICK: I guess. Plus, reefer's real expensive, so—]

JO-LYNNE: So I thought to myself—you know, after seeing you—that maybe I could convince you that this was a terrible, terrible thing that he had done, and that maybe I could offer you enough so that you'd take the risk, and then maybe you'd help me. Maybe you'd do this for me. Because it wasn't just an argument, you see? This man—Curtis Lowe—he set him up. He hated my husband and insulted him and taunted him and called the police on him and...just *wouldn't* leave him *alone!* He forced him outside. He forced him to try something. To go after him. So now...after the police and the court and everyone says he was innocent, and he goes back into that house and eats and sleeps and lives his life like nothing happened...I can't breathe. I feel him all the time. I feel him like it's a fever on my skin, and I can't...I mean, I try to...*(Pause. She takes a step away. Stops.)* Excuse me a second, OK?

[CHICK: Take your time. *(He watches her a moment. He then removes a darkly stained rag from his back pocket. He moves behind her and offers it to her.)* Here you go. *(She stares at the rag.)* It's clean, It's just that the stains don't wash out.]

(She takes it from him. Faces him.)

JO-LYNNE: Is this something you would do, do you think?

By the Sea: Dusk
Terrence McNally

Dana: a jogger at beach
Scene: Dusk

Dana attempts conversation with jogger, Willy—he jogs off—she responds.

○   ○   ○

Dana: Don't let it go to your head! I say hello to everyone! I even talk to total assholes like you.
(To audience.)
Why did I have to tell him that? What business of his is it why I do this? I do this because I'm worried I'm getting a big ass. I don't think he's worried he's getting a big ass. It was small talk. I'm not very good at it. So take me out there and feed me to the sharks! I hate small talk. There should be a federal law against it. All I had to say was "Hi, I'm Dana. I think you're very attractive and you look like someone I used to know and if you're not, I still think you're very attractive and I would very much like to sleep with you, I think, and I wonder what you think of women who say things like that, so let me re-phrase all that and ask you if you're ever so lonely, so achingly lonely, that your ass could be as big as China and you wouldn't give a damn or that you would like to walk out into that surf there and start swimming and swim and swim and swim and swim until you couldn't anymore and you went under and you finally took that one big breath that would fill your lungs with water and have you ever wondered what it would be like to go that way? No, Dana, darling, I don't think that's a good opening conversational gambit either. Tell him he looks like Willy Bukowski, someone you went to high school with and had a big crush on in the 11th grade before you moved to Ohio and never got over. It's a small world, but not that small. Not that small. It never was, never will be. I don't know why I keep doing this. It's not my ass I should be worried about.

A Candle in the Window
Tom Gilroy

MADDY: a woman who has picked up a man at a bar, intelligent and perceptive, 42
SCENE: The suburban northeast

Following a night out on the town, Maddy has brought home John, a frightening volatile ex-Marine who turns violent when their sex play goes awry. When John threatens her physically, Maddy demonstrates a streak of nihilism that makes her fearless.

MADDY: *(Slaps him harder.)* Why not? What are you going to do? Kill me? Beat me up? Big fuckin' deal! I'm gonna die? Big fuckin' deal! You're gonna do it? Not in a million years, Buckwheat. If you think for one second I believe you have the balls to beat the shit out of me until I'm unconscious, or strangle me—which takes about ten minutes, by the way—if you think I believe you have the balls to sit there and strangle me or beat me for *ten full minutes,* realize what you've done, feel *guilty,* erase all your fingerprints, get dressed, take your knapsack and start hitchhiking at four in the fucking morning, get arrested, *lie* in court, go through a whole fucking *trial* lying, and then get the chair or life in prison, then you are fucking out of your mind. You don't have the balls to go through with it. You'd crack and you know it. You'd confess and say 'It wasn't the real me' or 'I was drunk, but now I'm in AA' and fuckin' cry your eyes out and you know it. And you don't have the balls.
(A pause.)
So spare me the threats about your mysterious and dangerous past and all the things I don't know, okay? Because I just don't give a shit about your past. I have a past, too, you know. Everybody does. I met you in a bar, I liked you, I took you home. It's not a fucking classic novel or something, okay?

A Cheever Evening

A.R. Gurney

ALICE: an economically frustrated woman, 30s
SCENE: America in the 50s and 60s

The success of her friends drives Alice into a fit of pique while sharing perfume in the powder room.

○   ○   ○

ALICE: Scary hell. You're very, very lucky. You don't know how lucky you are. *(Brushing her hair angrily.)* I have this cake of soap. I mean, I *had* this cake of soap. Somebody gave it to me when I was married. Some maid, some music teacher. It was good English soap, the kind I like, and I decided to save it for when Larry made a killing and could take me to Bermuda. First I thought I could use it when he got the job in Hartford. Then when we went to Boston. And then, when he got work here, I thought maybe this time, maybe *now* I get to take the kids out of public schools and pay the bills and move out of those second rate rentals we've been living in. Well last week, I was looking through my bureau drawers, and there it was, this cake of soap. It was all cracked, so I threw it out. I threw it out because I knew I never was going to have a chance to use it. I'm never going to Bermuda. I'm never even going to get to Florida. I'll never get out of hock, ever, ever, *ever.* For the rest of my life, for the rest of my *life,* I'll be wearing ragged slips and torn nightgowns and shoes that hurt. And every taxi driver and doorman and headwaiter in this town is going to know in a minute that I haven't got five bucks in this black imitation-suede purse that I've been brushing and brushing and brushing for the past ten years. *(She sits down next to Laura.)* How do you rate it, Laura? What's so wonderful about you that you get a break like this? *(She runs her fingers down Laura's arm.)* Can I rub it off you? Will that make me lucky? I swear to Jesus I would murder somebody if I thought it would bring us any money. I'd wring somebody's neck—yours, anybody's—I swear to Jesus I would—! *(She stops herself.)* Well anyway. Thanks for the *Taboo. (She hurries off.)*

A Cheever Evening
A.R. Gurney

Christina's high level of energy helps to distance her from the empty nature of her life. Here, she describes her technique for relaxation.

O　　　O　　　O

CHRISTINA: *(To audience.)* Lately my husband and I have had trouble getting to sleep. Burt is temporarily unemployed, so he relaxes by taking long walks around the neighborhood. As for me? Why I simply review what I've done during the course of the day. This morning, for example, I drove Burt to the early train so he could look for another job. Then I...*(Consults her notebook.)* Had the skis repaired. Booked a tennis court. Bought the wine and groceries because tonight was our turn to give the monthly dinner of the Société Gastronomique du Westchester Nord. Attended a League of Women Voters meeting on sewers. Went to a full-dress lunch for Bobsie Neil's aunt. Weeded the garden. Ironed a uniform for the part-time maid who helped with the dinner. Typed two and half pages of my paper for the Book Club on the early novels of Henry James. Emptied the wastebaskets. Helped the sitter prepare the children's supper. Gave Ronny some batting practice. Put Lizzie's hair in pin curls. Got the cook. Met Burt at the five-thirty-five. Took a bath. Dressed. Greeted our guests in French at half past seven. Said *bon soir* to all at eleven. And that's about it. *(Puts her notebook away.)* Some people might say I am prideful for accomplishing all this. I don't think so. All I really am is a woman enjoying herself in a country that is prosperous and still young. *(Burt comes on, again in dark clothes.)* Coming to bed, darling?

Collateral Damage
Mansel Robinson

HAN: a North American Native, 20-25
SCENE: A prison

Han is being held in a mysterious prison with no true knowledge of her captors or the crime with which she has been charged. To help pass time, she and her fellow prisoners play a game in which each person tries to create a movie script based on three pre-assigned words. The following western fantasy is what Han is able to make from "poachers," "clinical," and "dig."

O   O   O

HAN: Poachers. That's a western. Cowboys and Indians. *(She takes a moment, then starts in.)* We hike above the rain, the clouds draped like scarves around the throat of the mountains.

[HENRY: Hey, you're good.]

HAN: We are in the middle of history. Below us, a thousand-year-old forest, an endless cycle of generation and regeneration. Above us, a 747 full of tourists claws a white scar across the face of the sky, less a scar really than a thin line of cocaine, one quick rush in the brain of modern man, a quick expensive buzz of euphoric desolation. But we aren't here for the Nikon snaps, we aren't tourists, we're on a mission, an action, we are underground above the clouds. Three nights previous, my partner had spotted their camp-fire. Poachers, looking for bear. We've been tracking them for seventy-two hours. They're good woodsmen, they move quickly, when we come across their campsites the fire is wet and dead. Considerate poachers. On the morning of the third day, we are close. We spot them occasionally with the rifle scope. My partner says they look like political aides on a camping week-end, clinical professionals. We follow up. Up. Up. Up. We hear the first shot echo down the valley. I raise my rifle scope in time to see the bear come up on her hind legs, pawing the air, her mouth and jaw shot away. *(She uses Jeanne to illustrate the story.)* The second shot catches her in the throat, the third in her lungs. I think I hear the bear scream. She raises the gore of her face to the sky and topples over a small ravine. She bounces once, twice and is still. We reach the spot an hour later. The poachers are gone. *(Pause.)* I've made a mistake. The poachers weren't trophy hunters after all. *(Pause.)*

They're after something else. There is a single slice in the belly. The gall bladder has been removed. It will be dried and powdered and sold as an aphrodisiac. In a small shop just outside the financial district, brokers will buy it by the gram. Of all the secrets of the east, thirty centuries of science and thought, this is all that the brokers have bothered to learn. The ravens begin to circle. My...partner...begins to dig.

Collateral Damage
Mansel Robinson

JEANNE: Franco-Ontarian, 30-35
SCENE: A prison

Jeanne and her husband, Henry, have been held without charge for several weeks in a mysterious prison. The claustrophobic confines of their physical and emotional space is beginning to affect their relationship in a negative way. When Jeanne realizes that Henry still carries adolescent prejudice against Franco-Canadians in his heart, she does her best to punish him with the following revelation.

○　　　○　　　○

JEANNE: On the day of my wedding I drive with my father over the river to the church. He stops at the dairy and buys us popsicles. We drive around town until the popsicles are finished, like when I was younger. He does not say anything about the English boy waiting in the church. He tells me that I look like my mother. We go inside the church. Remember the words of the minister? "Wilt thou love him, comfort him, honour, and keep him, in sickness and in health; and forsaking all other, keep thee only unto him, so long as you both shall live?" *(Pause.)* Do you like those words, Henry? *(Silence.)* At the reception: arctic char, wild rice, pickerel sushi, Canada goose pâté, seapie, tourtière, sugar pie. The friends of the groom sit on one side. Friends of the bride the other. The liquor begins to dilute the centuries of animosity between our two little solitudes. The band plays a slow one. My new father-in-law asks me to dance.

(She pulls Han onto the dance floor.)

He pulls me close. It is our fourth slow one. His breath is hot in my face. His eyeballs boil in rye and 7-Up. He smiles at me. He pulls me closer.

(They dance very close.)

He says to me. Softly, "French girls. You really like it eh?" I can feel the telescope between his legs. "You come and see me any time you get lonely," he says. "But your son," I start to say, "My son," he smiles, "my son is irrelevant."

Company Policy
Michael Ajakwe Jr.

ANNE MARIE GARRETT: a corporate VP, 30s
SCENE: Corporate offices

Anne Marie's authority has been usurped by a male co-worker. Here, she bemoans the system that has led her to the "glass ceiling."

O   O   O

ANNE MARIE: Ever wake up and feel like you should've never got out of bed? Well, this is one of those days. *(Beat.)* Got two new agents starting today. Actually, I hired one and *he* hired the other. Not that I mind. After all, it is his company. Nevermind that, as Vice President, it's my job to recruit new agents. I mean, I am capable of making those kinds of decisions unassisted, thank you. I am a college graduate, thank you. I do have an MBA from UCLA, thank you. And I do have 10 years of experience telling people how to think, what to do, and where the hell they can go if they don't want to do it, thank you very much. *(Beat.)* No, I don't mind. Hey, I'm a team player. And if the boss wants to play catch, I'll get a glove. I have six big burly, rough-and-ready older brothers so I know how to hang with the boys. Be one of the guys. "Fuckin' A!!" *(Beat, sulking.)* I know it's because I'm a woman. If I was a man, he would've *never* entered my space. Don't get me wrong. I'll always be grateful to Sam for giving me an opportunity few women in corporate America ever get. I went from Agent to V.P. in less than two years. And you know, not once did he ever hit on me. But sometimes, even the most open-minded men can be sexist pigs. *(Beat.)* The bottom line is, I hired the best person for the job. It just so happens that he happened to be a man, a Black man, a gorgeous Black man who, I might add, is brilliant. At least on paper. Or maybe it was those sexy brown eyes that kept saying, "Yes, hire him! He's the one! He's the one!" *(Catching herself.)* I can't believe I'm acting this way over a man, a Black man. I don't even like Black men. Not that I don't like them, I've just never been attracted to them. Black men or Asian men. But there was something different about this one. Something I've never felt before when it comes to "them." He moved me in his interview. I was so turned on after he left, I thought I was going to explode. I couldn't wait to call and tell him he had the job. *(Smiles.)* That's why I told him before he left. *(Frowns.)* Then that bitch walked in. I don't care where she went to school or how many degrees she has or how she was wearing the hell out of that grey suit—she was a bitch. One of those Black American Princess with an attitude. Sam didn't think so, though. He walked in just when I was sending Little Miss Black America on her merry way. They talked for…couldn'tve been more than two minutes. Small talk. Shop talk. Bull shit! Two minutes and he's "impressed." He wants to give her a second interview, personally. I remind him that we only need one person. Hello…! We're already over budget for this fiscal year. He doesn't care. He wants her. *(Shrugging, with a grin.)* What could I do? He's the boss. And what the boss wants, the boss gets. Hey, if it makes him happy, I'm happy. *(Frowning.)* Ambulance-chasing flirt! *(Composing herself.)* Come on, Anne Marie. Get a grip. It's against company policy to bad-mouth a co-worker, even if it's true. Remember, we're one big happy family.

Company Policy
Michael Ajakwe Jr.

A. LaShaun Lee: a woman starting a new job, 20-30
Scene: Corporate offices

Here, a very driven young black woman prepares to begin a new job in white corporate America.

○   ○   ○

LaShaun: What're you looking at? Never seen a Black woman in a suit before? *(Takes stapler out and puts it on her desk.)* I talk a lot a shit, don't I? And we just met. *(Beat.)* Bitch! There. Now we can be friends. I'm A. LaShaun Lee and you're…obviously bored or have nothing better to do with your time otherwise you wouldn't be here, right? *(Smiles.)* I'm always like this when I start a new job. I think it has something to do with that time of the month. I always start *before* my period instead of *after* my period. I know it shouldn't make a difference, since it's going to come regardless, but for some reason I feel so much better after it's been here than when it's on its way. Can any of you ladies out there relate to what I'm saying? *(Takes out pencil sharpener.)* I'm sure some of you men out there can relate too. You know who you are. Be mad for no reason. Just upset…for nothing. At least for us, it only happens once a month. Ya'll get the fever twice a month. *(Takes out calendar.)* And you never miss. It's either the first or the fifteenth. I don't know why Mr. Churchill hired me. I wasn't even really looking for a job. Hell, I had a job. A good one. I was just looking around. You know, shopping. Next thing I know, I'm putting in my two weeks and telling everybody to kiss my ass. Felt good, too. Especially that damn underwriter who was always rubbing up against me, talking about "Uh, excuse me LaShaun." Hallway is five-feet wide and he's excusing himself. Who do I look like, Heidi Fleiss? I know a feel when I feel one. I slapped that old fool so hard he started speaking in tongues. I told him, I don't play that. Keep your hands to yourself or lose 'em. Mama didn't raise no slut. *(Takes out handcuffs.)* What are these doing in here? *(Puts handcuffs back in box.)* I hope this job works out, though. Mr. Churchill says it's a place where I can grow because it's small, I'm smart and he's the boss. But you never know when it comes to White men. He could just be saying that because he knows that's what I wanna hear or because I make his company look good or because he feels guilty for all the niggas he never hired when he should've or because he wants to screw me. Take your pick. Not that his "Girl Friday," Ms. My-Shit-Don't-Stink, is any better. I know, if she had it her way, I wouldn't be here, even though I've probably got more education than she does. How many Black women do you know with undergraduate degrees from Berkeley and *two* graduate degrees from Stanford *(Frowning.)* ...yet are only good enough to come in as a manager-in-training. *A manager-in-training?* It's company policy, they said. Company policy my tit. I could probably run this motherfucker myself. I've got five years experience with the number-two insurance company in the world and was basically running my unit by myself. *(Smiles.)* You should've seen the look on the faces of "Honkey-Dee" and "Honkey-Dum" when I was Agent of the Month five months in a row. They had no choice but to promote me and give me my own office. I can't lie, they treated me real good. Like a queen. When I told them I was leaving, some of them even cried. 'Specially the old White ones. Yep, they loved them some LaShaun. I never spread my legs for any of them. I just did my job, did it well, and didn't let anybody walk over me. I guess you could say they respected me, my work ethic. And, you know, it's rare when you can work with a bunch of people and be liked *and* respected. *(Takes out name-plate.)* Who am I kidding? I know they all wanted to sleep with me. Even the women. *(Beat.)* They even told me that if I didn't like it here, I could come back and they would rehire me, no questions asked. How's that for Black Power? *(Throws fist in the air and bows her head à la Black Power Salute.)* I don't know why those White folks loved me so much. I must be Tomming somehow. Maybe I talk too White or I walk too White or I act too White. Yeah, maybe I'm not Black enough 'cause White folks ain't supposed to love niggas as much as they love me. *(Takes out a stack of books.)* That's why I got my *Black Revolutionary Guide* right here, my *Book of Black Quotations* and my *Autobiography of Malcolm X.* Can't go nowhere without my Malcolm. I even have a copy in the glove compartment of my car. Nope, I ain't no sellout. I'm a Black woman on a mission called S-U-C-C-E-S-S. That's right, I will not be denied. I'm gettin' mine "by any means necessary." Don't get me wrong. The road to the presidency ain't no cakewalk but, as Frederick Douglass once said, "If there is no struggle, there is no progress." *(Takes out a framed photo of Frederick Douglass and puts in on her desk.)*

Crow

Louis Nowra

CROW: a black woman fighting to keep her land, 40s
SCENE: Darwin, Australia, 1942

When Crow's white husband dies, she can not by law inherit the tin mine that they worked together. The determined woman approaches a local judge and demands that he make an appeal on her behalf. When he speaks coarsely of her mixed marriage, Crow angrily denounces his provincial racism.

◯　　　◯　　　◯

CROW: Don't you ever say that.

[THOMPSON: What?]

CROW: That word.

[THOMPSON: What word?]

CROW: About blacks and whites living together.

[THOMPSON: You mean combo?]

CROW: That Compound is filled with kids white fellas created. Yet all a man's got to do is just live with a blackwoman and you all laugh at him, turn your back on him—cos he's living out in the open, living honest. Everyone turned their back on Patrick, cause he was with me—living in the open—you did too—

[THOMPSON: *(exasperated)* For God's sake, Crow…]

CROW: No, you all looked down on him and me. When he went to have a drink at the pub, no one would serve him. Yet all those men go slinking around creating all those kids in the Compound. We were allright out there by ourselves. I mean, he wasn't perfect, being a man, being Irish and all that—I mean, I used to think blackfellas were bullshitters until I ran into a few Irish fellas. Christ, they lay it on thick. He called me a goddess, a black Madonna, the fire of his loins—and that was only on the first date! I have Vince by him and think, well, it's all fine and dandy, he's working at the abattoirs, and next moment he's saying he's bought a gold mine—for peanuts. I did cause to utter, Mr. Thompson, such pearls of wisdom as, 'Why would anyone sell a goldmine for peanuts?' But would he listen? He spent every penny on it. We go out there in the backblocks, we go inside with a torch

and there it is—the whole cave sparkling like the milky way. Well, we're laughing and dancing and crying, deciding what dreams to make real…when a piece of gold falls on me. Just a flake, then another flake. The fella who sold it to us had done the old trick, put some gold in a shotgun and peppered the mine shaft…so we were left with a useless mine. So he drinks for a week, singing those sad Irish songs, don't the Irish have any happy ones? I nearly throttled him. Then some old prospector comes by and spots something and says, 'That's tin'. So, it's party time again. We didn't realize it would be all backbreaking toil for years. Everyone talking about us here back in Darwin—Pat living with me and not hiding it. But we eventually made a living, nothing grand, but it was an honest living, Mr. Thompson.
(Pause.)
I worked every day for that mine, it's mine and our son's.
(She downs the beer.)
Thanks for the beer.

Dates and Nuts
Gary Lennon

EVE: very excitable. Hyper. She has a tough edge. Wild. 30s
SCENE: New York City

The bombastic Eve has been stood up by a man she has dated only once before. Here, she offers a scathing review of their disastrous date.

○   ○   ○

EVE: No, no, no, I'm ah…I'm going to wait 'til you finish and you guys can drive me home. I have to tell you, Mary, I am angry. I'm angry. I'm not only angry, I'm furious. I thought that Vinny and I had a good time. Sort of.
[MARY: He told me he did too.]
EVE: He said that, did he? We went to the theater, laughed a little. He slept over. I heated up some rigatoni. I made homemade sauce and meatballs. Lots of garlic. I made garlic bread. He said he liked it. We played around. Quickly showered. Then he insisted on posing for me, showing me his body-building routine. Then he said he was in the mood to watch a movie. It was the first time I ever heard porno movies called "progressive culture videos"…See Vinny is an Italian bodybuilder from California. I told him I didn't have any. He almost cried. He told me he didn't think he could get excited—get off again, the exact words—without the movie. That made me feel good, very close to him. He showed me his whole weightlifting routine using my end table and the lamps for weights, and I didn't say anything. He was very self-indulgent, and I didn't say anything. He never asked me a question. Ah, I'm lying. He did ask me a question. He asked me two. He asked me how much I weighed and what was the percentage of body fat on my body. These are two very unpopular questions to ask me, OK? I don't think just me, but any woman. This was before he asked me if he could use me as a weight to lift over his head because he was starting to resent me for missing his workout that night. He wanted to do triceps. He proceeded to finish his workout at my house using me as an inanimate object—a barbell, OK? He was lifting me above his head and dipping me behind his neck. I let it go. I tried to understand. Then he asked me if he could borrow thirty dollars so

he could buy his amino fuel, which is an integral part of his workout or he couldn't sleep over. A threat. I told him I did not have any money because I had spent all my money on the cabs…and groceries. OK! Then he proceeded to remind me that I had a Citibank card in my wallet, which he must have seen when I paid for the theatre tickets with my charge card because he forgot his gym bag at home with his wallet in it, convenient, which depressed him and which is why I tried to cheer him up for two hours prior to our sexual intercourse, which proved to be not thrilling. Anyway, he informed me that if I would lend him the money he would pay me back tonight here in the club in more ways than one. And, as you see, this will never happen. I am a manatee!

[MARY: Eve, I gotta go in the back. I gotta sing.]

EVE: *(Calmly.)* You do that…don't worry about me. I'm OK If Vinny comes here, I will kill him. I will go to jail, but I will kill him first. Yes, I will.

Dates and Nuts
Gary Lennon

EVE: very excitable. Hyper. She has a tough edge. Wild. 30s
SCENE: New York City

Eve has finally met a man she just might be able to love. On their two-week anniversary, Eve takes a chance and tells him of her life in the lonely years before they met.

○   ○   ○

EVE: You know, it's funny that you say I'm like a snowflake, 'cause I've always felt like one...no, no...I'm serious. It's like you read my mind or something sometimes.

[AL: Yeah.]

EVE: Yeah, my whole life. I've always felt like this little snowflake in this big snowstorm being pushed this way and that way by the wind. You know, the whole time I was out there looking to meet somebody, I felt like I was this snowflake that was looking to meet, or...or...land on another snowflake so that I could finally make snow. You know, be snow...or something...you know what I mean...I'm weird.

[AL: No, no, I know what you mean. G'head.]

EVE: I don't know...It seemed like I was the type of flake that always landed on someone's nose and melted by itself before I met another one...I never sort of like...hit the ground with the others...and then you came along and the storm sort of settled, and I guess we're making snow or something...I don't know...We're a weird couple, Al. You know, before you, I used to stalk love late at night. I used to get lonely about three o'clock in the morning. So, I'd take my bike out and ride the streets to see if anybody was still out, anybody drunk enough or stoned enough, or innocent enough to want to take me home. The streets were my haven, I didn't like bars because you had to talk in bars, and that was asking too much of me. I was desperate, I guess. I wasn't stalking love. I was stalking sex, something dark, something dense to fill the emptiness...death really. I was stalking death. I wanted something to numb my loneliness, to fill the empty hole inside me, and by accident I found you. I'm lucky. When I was out there, I'd always meet someone who had the same desperate look in their eyes. I called it the "hunger." There are a lot of hungry people out there still looking. Hunting. It's an unmistakable look, a glance, a stare that only those of us out there know. The lonely. The hungry. I was dying of loneliness, and you saved me from the rest of it. On our two-week anniversary, I want you to know how grateful I am that I have you. I'm lucky.

A Dead Man's Apartment
Edward Allan Baker

NICKIE: 38
SCENE: Providence, 1994

Nickie arrives at the home of her lover, Lonnie, and practices telling her husband she wants out.

○   ○   ○

NICKIE: Today's the day, Lonnie. I can't do this anymore. I can't pretend that I believe somethin that I don't cause a the kids yunno, they been in the way an I I don't want to be with you anymore, next to you, callin you or ironin your shirts or cookin meals. *(She has backed Lonnie to the coach. She rips off her hat, glasses, and smock. Drops her pocketbook.)* I'm at a place that is kinda hard to explain but I know it's the end of something and I want to get out before I reach forty, okay? I feel sick inside cause of it every day an an at night I sit on the edge of the bed an I see your shape an I hear you snorin and I grab by Saint Jude Medal and I pray for strength, for help, and I say *"Get me the fuck out of this mess!"* I I say it with tears in my eyes and I say it really pissed off an I say it every night. I I have to say it'd be easier in a way if you hit me and the kids but you never did an you always get your ass outta bed in the mornin to go to work to pay the bills...it's just that um...that I don't feel anything deep for you *and I'm so fuckin' bored I could die, do you understand?!*
(Lonnie stirs to get up. She waves him off.)
NICKIE: Wait wait...*(Beat.)* Where are we goin? I'm afraid and I just want to snap my fingers an go forward five years or back twenty. I for a long time have felt my weddin ring is around my neck an gettin tighter an tighter an...
[LONNIE: *(Rises.)* Okay Nickie, I...]
NICKIE: *Let me go! Just let me go!* Please say "It's all right, I understand, have a good life, good luck, and good-bye." An then just go. Walk away. No no tears. No anger. No hurt feelings. Just...walk...away...from me...

Demons
Robert Brustein

LAURA: an unhappy spirit, 30-40
SCENE: Cambridge, MA

Laura has been summoned back to earth by her husband, who fancies himself a modern Faust; sacrificing all to be reunited with his one true love. Here, Laura angrily confronts Peter with the fact that she died childless—at his insistence.

○   ○   ○

LAURA: What do you think it's like for a woman to go through life without a baby? Blocked from a basic female function? Filling the emptiness in health spas and exercise salons, reading fashion magazines?

[PRIDEAU: You say you've become a feminist. Don't you people hold that careers and homemaking don't mix?]

LAURA: You people? You people? Why do *you* people always have to classify other people. We're not "you people," we're humans—like you. Of course we want to lead our own lives. We have talents like everyone else. But we were also made to have children—little ones, not big grownup infants looking for lifetime breastfeeding.

[PRIDEAU: *(Sadly.)* I've already admitted I wanted you all to myself, for all of my life. I loved you.]

LAURA: Egoism. Selfishness. Narcissism. My case is proved, you self-centered fathead. Don't you know that "all of life" is nothing but a blink in time? If you lived to be a hundred, your term on earth would still only be a passing sigh. You should have given life to children. Let me show you the son we might have had. This would have been your immortality.

(Images of a lovely blond boy from infancy to adulthood appear on screen as she describes him.)

I would have called this baby Luke. Look, he has your eyes. Isn't he darling? Healthy, bright, and touched with grace. Look at that golden smile, those little dimpled fingers. How I would have loved to bathe him, change his diapers, oil and powder his tushie. A brand-new baby offers so much possibility—purity and innocence and hope. He died before he lived, a sacrifice to the miracle of birth control.

[PRIDEAU: *(Hurt to the quick.)* Don't!]

LAURA: *(Ignoring him, as the pictures show a child growing from infancy to manhood.)* He's seven now. Winters of snowballs and sledding, summers of scooters, snorkels, sailboats, ragtag. Should he spend vacations with us or go to camp? Now he's twelve. Private schools or public? He's fully grown now. What college? What career? He would have been an artist, married a loving woman, raised beautiful children. Grandchildren for your old age. Blocked by the rubber pocket of an interuterine device. Because of you. You killed your child. You killed the children of our child.

[PRIDEAU: For love of you.]

LAURA: No. For love of yourself. *(Crying.)* Where are my babies? My sweet small things? My life? My hopes? Without them, I'm nothing. And so are you. A broken synapse in the brain of time.

Dog Opera
Constance Congdon

MADELINE: a good blue-collar catholic girl raised in Queens who made the long trip into Manhattan to go to NYU so she could have an interesting life, 30s
SCENE: Here and now

Here, Madeline takes a moment to confront a statue of the Virgin Mary with the fact that she hasn't been able to forgive her for abandoning her in a time of great need.

◯   ◯   ◯

MADELINE: I know we haven't had a good relationship since that time in high school when, I felt, you really let me down. I guess I let you down, too. I just expected you to understand since you had been in the same position.

I waited in the backyard all night, on the terrace, and you never came, I never got a single feeling, no message, nothing—just the big cosmos, surrounded by a circle of orange from the lights off the avenue, just all that black sky with those holes of light staring back at me. I begin to feel like Sereta Lopez was right, that we were all just bugs inside a really big coffee can with a black plastic lid that some little mean white boy was keeping and he poked holes in the lid just to let us breathe a little and those holes let in light and we thought they were stars.

So I had the abortion, Mary, and I never needed to use birth control again. And Pete was the one who drove me there and back and talked to me while I lay in the backseat with a towel between my legs because fucking Ray— that's what we always called him after that—that was his generic name because that pretty much defined him—Fucking Ray wanted nothing to do with it since he was ashamed of knocking up a fat girl. And it was Pete who got me back into the house and sat up and drank with my mother who thought I was just broken-hearted over some guy which I was, but I was also mourning my womb which was pretty much a goner, too. And after that, Ray's Camarro had its headlight busted out about six times a year by an unknown vandal in various locations around the city until Fucking Ray got married and moved to Sparta. And Pete stopped carrying a hammer in his bookbag.

As you can tell, I'm still pissed that I never heard from you.

You would not believe the world, Blessed Mother. And from whatever place you see it—those mountaintops in Yugoslavia which doesn't exist anymore, by the way—from those tacos and potato chips and tree trunks that people see you in—from wherever—you must have noticed how really like the Last Day it is.

So I'm just here to let bygones be bygones, and to ask you to please protect Peter.

I forgive you, by the way, wherever you are.

(Looking up at the heavens.)

For godssake, I know this is just a bunch of plaster here.

(Madeline crosses herself—exits.)

Dog Opera
Constance Congdon

BERNICE: a tough old broad; irascible and matter-of-fact, 60s
SCENE: Here and now

Bernice has fallen in her bathroom. Here, she contemplates her predicament before calling for help.

○   ○   ○

BERNICE: I've sifted through my life and I can't find a single reason why I should be lying here on my own bathroom floor while my sister Bea is happily married for the third time in San Diego. But, you know, I bet anything, I bet you fifty dollars that she will be nursing him in six months and spending her hard-earned dollars on a hefty nurse to lift him in and out of the bathtub. Men are such weaklings. How they got control of the world I don't know. It's because women have no guts and are afraid to make anybody mad because they hate to be alone. And how do most of them end up? Alone! Ow. Ow. 'Course what do I know, I'm lying on my own bathroom floor.

Don't you know that when they find me, some young prick is gonna say, "She's fallen and she can't get up." Oh, the young. I'm so jealous of them. The beautiful are cruel and stupid—there's no doubt about it.

I'm glad I went to the mall and got a decent bathroom rug the last time. Bathrooms always remind me of confessionals. Not that our confessional was ever tiled. But I did feel sitting in there with the priest like we were on a two-holder—a kind of really nice one with walls to separate the sexes and a little grate to talk through, like they might of had in Venice. Although I suspect most people just went in the canals. Oh, we're a dirty bird, mankind. Dirty, dirty— *(Sees something.)* —I've got to tell Henreeka to do a better job on this floor, particularly around this bathtub.

It's strange I'm not in more pain. Maybe I've had a stroke. Oh god, I'll be a vegetable!

Wait a minute—I'm talking. Vegetables don't talk, old girl.

I'm dead. I just *think* I'm talking, and I'm actually—

HELLLLLP! HELLLLLLLLLLP! HELLLLLLPPP!

Down By The Ocean

P.J. Barry

LIL: a woman caring for her husband, a stroke victim, 50-60
SCENE: A summer cottage in Rhode Island, 1960s

Lil and Peter have returned to their beach house the summer following Peter's stroke. Here, Lil does her best to catch Peter up on family news.

○   ○   ○

LIL: *(Setting him in place.)* Isn't it a perfect day? Just perfect! *(Pause.)* I'm so glad I got my swim in. You know me. I have to get my swim in or I'm not happy. *(Sits at a TV table with string beans, a pot, etc.)* I'll bet they're all in again…at least Ann and Betsy. Not Alice, of course. You know what she's doing, the scamp. *(Laughs, strings beans.)* You comfortable, honeybun? *(Pause.)* Good. *(Pause.)* You are my honeybun…always…always…*(Sings.)* Always. *(Smiles.)* On our honeymoon…that's when you first called me honeybun…I stole it from you. *(Pause.)* I was so frightened. I kept talking…chatter, chatter, chatter…and you said: "Stop talking, honeybun…just kiss me"…and I heard you take off your glasses and then you kissed me. *(Giggles.)* Oh, you were so sweet…so loving…oh, my! *(Giggles again.)* You like it out here, don't you. Like David—God rest his soul. He loved this porch, too…loved the view…the way you do. *(Sighs.)* David and Connie both gone now—God rest their souls. So sad…*(Sings loudly.)* "Sad, sad and lonely… sad, sad and blue…" *(Now Peter is revived by Lil's singing.)* And so we bought their summer place for us and our children…but Lilly and hers…so far away. Why anybody would want to live in Michigan is beyond me. Oh, Peter, I seldom refer to them as Little Lil and Little Peter anymore. Aren't you proud of me? *(Pause.)* I know you are. At least Lilly gave us grandchildren. I don't think Peter ever will. He's only dated a handful of girls in the last seven or eight years. Let's see. There were four. Anita…Helen… Roberta…wait, I skipped one. It was an M. *(Beat.)* M…*(Beat.)* Maxine! Oh, Maxine was a thousand years ago…she spoke several languages…What a memory! Still. There is hope, honeybun. *(Peter begins to nod off to sleep again and soon succeeds.)* Last week when he wrote and said he was a volunteer for

Kennedy...well, I was overjoyed! Of course, he's attached himself to a losing battle, a Catholic can't win the Presidency. *But* from now until November our son will most likely meet some pretty girl, most likely Catholic...so many of those volunteers for Kennedy will be. *(Pause.)* Keep your fingers crossed. *(Stops stringing the beans. Sighs.)* You change their diapers and bathe them and powder them and kiss them and feed them...and change their diapers and bathe them and powder them...and sing to them...*(Slightly teary-eyed. Sings three lines of a lullaby. Pause.)* ...and then they talk...and walk...and they're in school...in college...and married...or whatever...and gone. *(Sings with more volume, awakening Peter.)* "Gone are the days...When our hearts were young and gay..." *(Pause. Thoughtfully.)* And here we are, sugarplum, together in our summer place which was to be for them and their children...*(Pause.)* They come back home so seldom...Little Lil...Little Peter...*(Resumes stringing beans. With practicality.)* We are selling. It's on the market, I told you. Isabelle, next door, made us an offer. She said she'd stop by this afternoon...to chat. *(Peter appears more interested.)* I've never liked that girl. She still flaunts herself. Oh, she does. *(Pause.)* She appears to be a good mother, but I'm afraid she's...*(Whispers.)*...basically a tramp. *(Turning to him.)* You know I wouldn't use that word unless I felt it was hitting the nail right on the head. *(Peter is managing a slight gesture.)* What is it? Is that sweater a little heavy now? *(Rises, goes to him.)* I think so. Well, we'll be rid of that problem in a jiffy, my handsome husband. *(Begins to get him out of it.)* Handsome, honeybun, sugarplum. You are. *(Kisses his cheek.)* I see the glint in your eye.

Drive Like Jackson Pollock
Steven Tanenbaum

CELINA: a cigar-smoking Latina hedonist, 20-30
SCENE: Here and now

Celina has struggled to stay "clean" ever since rehab. Here, the passionate young woman describes the experience that led her back to heroin use.

O   O   O

CELINA: I was hanging out in the park, listening to somebody's boombox. Had this hip hop thing going and I was bobbin' my head to the beat. But the music didn't engage my body…so, after a while, I moved on. Over the hill, an Asian man in coveralls was playing the violin for spare change. I stopped because there was something vaguely familiar about the music. After a moment, a grainy picture formed in my head of myself as a kid, sitting on a piano bench, feet dangling, trying to learn that very same composition. No matter how hard I had practiced, I could never really connect, heart-to-heart, with classical music. So, after a while, I moved on…and headed for the pond. Inside the gazebo, some Peruvian musicians—Indians—were playing Andean folk music, heavy on the windpipes. I wasn't there too long before I felt it. I mean, I'm not from Peru, but my whole body started to move and the next thing I knew, my posture had completely changed. I was stand-ing…I was standing…tall. My feet were firmly planted and my head was high in the air. In one moment, that music had stripped away all the bullshit I keep myself wrapped in. I hadn't felt like that since…Ever since rehab, I've been convinced it's better to be wrapped up like a fucking mummy: Well preserved, but dead inside. It became clear to me that those Indians were messengers and they were saying: Clean equals death…When I looked around at everybody in the park, they all looked like me before: lifeless. It gave me the creeps…so, after a while, I moved on. When I got home, I found Brando asleep in my bed. The sheets covered his entire body. The only part of him that I could see clearly were his eyes. As I watched him sleep, that Andean folk music reverberated in my ears; it was as if those Indians were right there in my room. The music became so powerful I'm sure Brando could hear it in his dreams; because he awoke with a look that I clearly rec-ognized. His eyes were imploring me and I knew exactly what they were ask-ing me to do.

THE EIGHT: *Reindeer Monologues*
Jeff Goode

DANCER: a reindeer
SCENE: The North Pole

When Santa is accused of sexual misconduct with Vixen, her sister reindeer, the tabloid press quickly descends upon the other reindeer for their comments. Here, Dancer shares her favorite Santa story.

○   ○   ○

DANCER: This is my favorite Santa Clause story.

When I first came up here after I was offered this position.
I had no idea this was a Christmas-related job.
And I was looking over my contract, which, of course,
said that we made this run on December 24th, right?
And I'm looking over my contract, and I said,
"What about vacation days?"
And he said,
"You only work one day a year,
you don't get vacation days."
And I said,
"What about sick days and maternity leave?"
And he said
"You don't get sick days, either."
and I said
"What happens if I'm sick on the 24th? Or I'm pregnant?"
And he kind of turned a little red and said,
"You will work the 24th in sickness and in health,
and if you want this job
you will not give birth
on or about the 24th of December."
And I thought, that's a bit fascist.
But I saw he was getting a little hot around the collar, so I said,
"Okay, fine."

—But secretly I was thinking, we'll just wait and see.
I mean,
if I come in here barfing my lungs out on the 24th
this guy's not going to make me strap on a harness
and fly around the world.
He's got his clients waiting all year for him to make one delivery,
who's gonna notice if it's postponed a day or two.—

So I'm thinking it over:
no sick days, no vacation days,
but it's only once a year,

and I'm looking at my calendar, and suddenly,
—in a moment of brilliance—
I realize that this is during the holidays.
So then I said,
"So, Mr. Claus
is this scheduled for
sometime around the 24th
most of the time?" And he said,
"No,
it's scheduled for exactly on the 24th
all the time."
And I said,
"Well, not *every* year."
And he said,
"Yes, every fucking year."
Well, I was getting a little pissed off now,
and I said, "Well **excuse me,** Mr. Claus,
but what happens when it falls during
Hanukkah?"
—And I thought that was a reasonable question
because most businesses will give you time off
to spend Hanukkah with your family.—
But he just started laughing that annoying laugh.
And then he said,
"Dancer,
one of my reindeer is a practicing Muslim.

And most of them are devout agnostics.
But on December 24th
you are all Unitarians.
Because on Christmas Eve
I need Christmas deer
to deliver Christmas toys
for Christmas Day."

Boy was I embarrassed.

Emma's Child

Kristine Thatcher

EMMA MILLER: 19, a birth mother
SCENE: Hospital, intensive care

Emma describes seeing the father of her son in a bar.

❍   ❍   ❍

EMMA: I still *had* 'em. So, at the bar, that night, I let him come on in the same old way. I didn't hear nothin' new, but, I was *seein'* for the first time since he dumped me. He was *some* frat rat, and I was just a local nuthin'. It was cold, and I was wearing' cutoffs, and, I don't know, he pissed me off. So, for no reason, alls a sudden, I open my bag and take out a xerox of Robin's footprints, and I put the paper down—bang—right there on the table. Jamie looked at it, and he stopped breathin', just like that. I told him I wasn't comin after nuthin'. And I told him what a poor condition his little boy was in. He listened, and he listened, and when he finally talked, he asked a lot of questions. I told him about you guys. I told him about the monitors, and the tubes, and the sirens. So, he starts snifflin' and cryin'. Give me a break! And he goes, "Can I come up with you some time and seeee little Robin?" And I'm like, you're kiddin' me! So, I say to him, I go, "No way. No way in this wide world will you ever lay eyes on that boy." I know he's the father, and he's probably got rights, but I don't want him near this child. And I don't think he'll sue me or nuthin'. But, even if he does, I won't have him around. Okay?

Emma's Child

Kristine Thatcher

JEAN FARRELL: 40, adoptive mother
SCENE: Hospital, intensive care

Jean is talking to the newborn, describing a school trip she had taken in tenth grade where she saw a mongoloid baby for the first time.

$\bigcirc$ $\bigcirc$ $\bigcirc$

JEAN: *(She gets up and leans into the isolette.)* We're going to try something here, Baby. "Pirates of the Caribbean" coming up. If you don't panic, I won't. If, at any point, you hate this, however, just call out, all right? Boom! Back in the old isolette, okay? *(She looks for Laurence.)* What a name for a bed. "Isolette." *(To the baby.)* You needn't look so all alone, Gummy. We have a certain amount of experience on which to draw. You're not the first. I met someone like you once before. It was during a field trip with Mr. Garchow *(Pronounced "Gar-shaw")* Tenth-grade social studies—to the Coldwater State Hospital. *(As she speaks she takes brand-new clothing out of a bag, and puts it away. She rips price tags from a few items. Then she takes Robin's dirty laundry from under the isolette, and stuffs it into her bag.)* My mother used to say they had "no business taking a bus full of children to that awful place." We went in single file from one ward to the next. My classmates and I were introduced to mongoloid babies, with their high-pitched cries; young women, tearing their hair and skins; and old men, deserted, wailing, clad only in diapers. To think she lived with those sounds day and night. By the time we bottlenecked, just outside her room, I couldn't keep my limbs still, or catch a decent breath. Just ahead, my friend, Bev Tucker, class vice president and future homecoming queen, turned to me with a sharp whisper: "My God, you won't believe this. Nine years old, and lying in a baby's crib. Wisps of hair, on a *horse's* head. Her eyes must be *five* inches apart. Pass it on. They have to turn her twice a day. Her name is Debbie. Pass it on." *(Beat.)* The sunlight streamed into her quiet bed as I came near. Out of the corner of my eye, I saw her awesome shape. *(She gently touches the child.)* Not unlike yours, my boy. I also saw she kept her eyes cast down as Bev went

35

by. I decided I wouldn't look, either, as I took my turn before her. And, then, we both surprised ourselves: she looked up, and I looked down. In that one moment, I saw her daring! I saw her humor, her sweet, forgiving soul. Never before had I seen a face so loving and open. I wonder, if she could see you now, what she would say to you. What wonderful thing would she say? I want to say it.

Emma's Child
Kristine Thatcher

JEAN FARRELL: 40, adoptive mother
SCENE: Hospital, doctor's office

Jean is arguing with Henry, her husband, to keep the mongoloid baby they would have adopted had it been born healthy. She declares her devotion to the child.

○   ○   ○

JEAN: *(She finds her position.)* I'm going to visit today, and again tomorrow, and the day after that, until they send him to Miserecordia. Then I will visit him at Miserecordia. Henry, you talk about the pain we felt, and it's true, we did. It's pain I gather you're still feeling. I'm not. Haven't you noticed? All gone. *He* did it. You're right, you do have a choice: you can come with me, and meet him, or you can go home, and hang on to your precious pain. I'd like your blessing, Hal, but if I don't get it, that's fine, too.

Emotions
Robert Coles

JEN: a young woman considering moonlight, 20s
SCENE: The US Virgin Islands, the present

While sharing a romantic moment with a friend, Jen reveals her occasional fear of moonlight.

◯   ◯   ◯

JEN: It makes me scared sometimes.

[ALLIE: Scared?]

JEN: Yeah. When it's spooky. When it's quiet. Like…if I worked the last shift and I leave, and I walk down the beach. It can be so quiet, after the band stops playing, after everyone has gone. But it's not romantic, just…strange. Scary. When it's bright, the moonlight heightens everything. Makes it larger, sharper. Magnifies its oddness. The shapes…are threatening. The stillness…ominous. You expect that…this is the moment when paradise will turn on you. Exact the price for itself. For your enjoyment of it. For its…passivity at your enjoyment. Your *using* of it. Suddenly, a shadow will…leap. Leap out. At you. It happened once. A shadow…it seemed an *enormous*…an enormous *shape* of something. The stillness, the oddness, and then…it leaped. Thrusted, darted, *pouncing,* I thought. I thought…it would *grab* me. Exact its price. But…but it…was—

[ALLIE: A shadow.]

JEN: A lizard. Maybe big, but…maybe…I don't know. I thought…but…I don't know. It wasn't leaping at me. It was running. Running *from* me. *It* was scared, too. Probably of me. Silly. I was silly. Does that sound silly?

Gunplay
Frank Higgins

WOMAN COP: 30-40
SCENE: Here and now

Here, a down-to-earth police officer entertains a writer with a few anecdotes and some hard-won wisdom.

O   O   O

WOMAN COP: You the guy my partner talked about? The writer?…Yeah, I'll talk to you. Whatta you wanna know?…Well the way I look at life, society is like…livin' in a big building. The rich live on the top floors, the poor live on the bottom floors, and only us cops travel to all the floors. Only cops see it all. What's your name? Frank? I'll tell you what, Frank; first month on the job I realized I was less a cop than a social worker. Guy's knocked his wife's teeth out. "You want us to file charges?" "No, I love him." "How many times he done this to you?" "Only two or three." Only time she's gonna stop lovin' him is when he shoots her dead.

My partner tell you I got suspended once? My first Christmas, D & D. Domestic disturbance. Guy and his wife decoratin' their tree and screamin' at each other. "What's the problem, folks?" "No problem, officer. I say we put the *angel* on top the tree; she wants the *star*. Tell her she's screwed." And the wife says, "We got *angels* on the tree *already*. And besides, the star is *symmetrical*." And I make a big mistake. They're not drunk, they're rich, they're *white*. I let my guard down. "Who *cares* if the star's symmetrical?" the guy says, "The star doesn't *mean* anything. An angel *means* something." "Didn't you ever hear of the star of the *East*? The star means *Christ* is coming!" I step between 'em to keep 'em apart. "Now c'mon, folks. You're botherin' your neighbors." "They *should* be bothered! Nobody's gonna look at this tree with that *star* on it and think the tree is sayin' Christ is comin'!" And inside I'm crackin' up coz this is like Jackie Gleason on *The Honeymooners*. "*Everybody* knows the star means Christ is comin'; *you'd* know *too* if you weren't so *stupid!*" Zip, the guy grabs my gun, pulls it out. "Don't you call me stupid, I love you, I'll blow your head off!" And we get to fightin' over my gun. We're rollin' all over the floor, and then she gets mad coz I'm hittin' her husband even though he just aimed a gun at her, so she jumps on top me too. So when my sergeant comes in as backup, there I am, my gun in the guy's hand, pointin' right in my face. "Now you tell the truth; when you look at that star do you think 'Christ is comin'?!"

Know my other mistake, Frank? I forgot it was Saturday night. Unless you live alone, the most dangerous place you can be on a Saturday night is your own home. You've had a drink, and most people drink more Saturday. And most murders are by friends or relatives. A spouse. You married, Frank?... Don't blame ya. I don't think I'll ever get married; I scare people off. All I have to do is tell 'em the truth; that you can sit here now and feel superior and say you'd never hurt anybody you love, but you don't know. Coz when you got love between two people, look out. People argue, take away guns. Take away love. You'll take away half the murders.

Half-Court
Brian Silberman

JOAN: a woman struggling to define her sexuality, 30s
SCENE: Here and now

Here, Joan confesses feelings of asexuality to a man that she is briefly considering going to bed with.

○   ○   ○

JOAN: You think it's easier for me? It isn't. You ask me and I have no conception of my own sexuality, none whatsoever. The fact that I have a name that is feminine and that I menstruate is about all I have to tell me that I'm female. In the last three years I've had sex with four men and two women and I found it so off-putting, so difficult to cope with…I found that I just retreated and retreated and retreated…I have no conception of falling in love at all. I don't understand it. I don't want to get married…or have children…but I do want something…some form of relationship…some kind of proof in the shape of a person that I'm making progress…that there's some kind of movement. But I have no idea whether that person would be male or female…even now…none whatsoever. Men in particular I treat like explosives, something I don't know anything about, but which I know is going to blow up. So, I just tiptoe around, hoping to God I'm not in the blast area when it goes off. I never know how to be with them. I have no idea. I just try to be what they seem to want me to be. I completely erase myself…and then go away feeling really…yuk! Because if one of them said, "Why don't I take you out to dinner?" or something like that, I'd just think, oh, he's fallen for the old cardboard cutout that I wheel out, that's what he wants. And with women…I turn to women sometimes. But…I don't know…there's something missing somehow…it's…not a completion…

[DAVID: I'm sorry. I talk too much. You didn't have to get into something you didn't—]

JOAN: By now, David…by now the pond is fished out and the people who are left behind are people like me. And I don't want another one like me.

(There is a long pause.)

Do you know why you like watching lesbians make love? Because to you, it's totally non-threatening.

If We Are Women
Joanna McClelland Glass

RACHEL: a well-educated woman, 60s
SCENE: Guilford, CT

Rachel has driven to Connecticut to be with Jessica, her ex-daughter-in-law, whose lover of eight years has died. Here, the acerbic Rachel muses over the oddity of offering comfort to the woman who left her son.

O   O   O

RACHEL: How odd, to be here now. To drive up, four hours from Pennsylvania, to be at her side in her hour of grief. But I came willingly, as I always have. I came after the divorce when she was alone with the children and struggling for money. I mended and patched, I made slipcovers to hide the damage of kids and cats. And after Fleming arrived, I still came. I cooked for the four of them, my daughter-in-law, my two grandchildren, and the landscape painter. I cooked the old, Jewish dishes they requested. Blintzes and borsht, latkes, kreplach, challa, hamantashen. My friends think I've kept this relationship alive for my grandchildren. They think, because I could see my son in the kids' faces, I wouldn't mind serving up latkes to the invading landscape painter. They're wrong.

There's something in her life that's forever…*(shrugging)*…magnetic. And, repellant. Magnetic because her writing is so mysterious. I've thought if I could locate the source, the wellspring that propels her pen, I, too, might write. Why can't I? I love language, I express myself well. Perhaps I know too much. I'd read all of Shakespeare by the time I was twenty. I've taught the classics, I've read reams of criticism. But when I sit down to blank paper, my pen is paralyzed. *(An introspective pause.)* Her source is her feelings. Deeply, zealously felt feelings. Her profession is, essentially, one of confession. That's what's repellant. It's not my pen that's paralyzed, it's me. I'm ill-at-ease with the zealously felt. Gerald was, too…not surprising. The hand that rocks the cradle. He learned at my knee that people impaled on their feelings never achieve maturity. And I was right. There is something severely…arrested about Jess.

How odd to be here now, while she mourns the man who wasn't my son.

Jaws of Life
Jocelyn Beard

KRISTEN: HIV positive, 16
SCENE: An AIDS clinic

Several years later, Kristen has developed AIDS. Following a hospitalization for pneumonia, Kristen again vents her spleen upon her therapist.

○   ○   ○

KRISTEN: Yeah, I'm still here. Surprised? My T-cells take a lickin' but I keep on tickin', right? *(Listens.)* Oh, you heard about that, huh? Well, so what? My mom is a colossal asshole these days. Here I am, dying—or so I thought—of p-fucking-monia, and she's gabbin' away and gabbin' away about high school graduation. Like I give a shit. My so-called friends stopped visiting me like, two years ago, so why should I care about their stupid graduation? *(Listens.)* Huh? Why? Because I didn't want to, that's why! Why should I finish high school? So my mother can hang a diploma on my grave? What, is there college in heaven?

(The father enters silently behind Kristen and stands, listening.)

KRISTEN: You know what? Why don't you just go fuck yourself, you arrogant sonofabitch! *(She rises and begins to pace.)* You know exactly Jack Shit about me and my disease. You think I don't see you, climbing into your little silver beemer every night at exactly 5:30? God forbid anyone should need to talk at 5:31, right? What do you, go home to your wife and kids; eat, watch TV; maybe add a chapter to that book I hear you're writing? I bet you figure you're gonna make a fortune offa us, right? Us poor little lost souls. AIDS babies. Make sure you get a picture of that kid in 1308—he's down for the count. 48 hours, max. Put him right on the cover and wrap the whole thing up in one of your little red ribbons—*Christ,* you make me wanna puke! *(Listens.)* I'm angry? What, you get paid, like, 80 thousand a year to make amazingly insightful observations like that? Well, guess again. I'm not angry—not even close. In fact, I'm ecstatic. Yeah, that's right: ecstatic. Why? I'll tell you why. Because I know something that you'll never know, that's why. I know exactly where, when and how I'm gonna die, asshole. The biggest mother questions in all our lives and for me, they're answered. Where: right here. When: oh, year...year and a half. How: Of the plague. Your plague. Your red ribbon plague. For you, Doctor Douchebag, these questions will never be answered. You'll be cruising home some night and *Wham!* Some drunk driver will nail you and the beemer and not even the jaws of life will be able to save your sorry ass. Think about that when you're writing your stupid book. At least we know. You know nothing. You...

Jaws of Life
Jocelyn Beard

KRISTEN: HIV positive, 16
SCENE: An AIDS clinic

A one-night stand has destroyed young Kristen's life. Here, she angrily confronts her clinic therapist with the fact of her forced mortality.

○   ○   ○

KRISTEN: Yeah, I'm going home tomorrow, so what? I mean, who cares? Not my mother, that's for sure. It's pretty obvious that she can't handle this. *(Pause.)* Can I? What, handle this? What difference does it make? What's to handle? I'm gonna die, right? *(Pause.)* My life? That's pretty funny, doc. My life. Why don't you tell me about my life? Why don't you tell me about all the parties I'll never go to and the boys I'll never date? Tell me, why dontcha, about the man I'll never marry and the children I'll never have, the house I'll never live in…tell me about the drugs and the needles and the hospitals and the doctors…tell me about what it's going to feel like to waste away until I'm nothing but bones—go on, tell me! *(Pause.)* My father? I don't know. I don't know if she told him yet. *(Pause.)* Why should I call him? He hasn't called me in five years. What is he gonna swing into my room on a vine or something? He's the last person I want in my life right now. *(Pause.)* Jason? *(Laughs.)* You've gotta be kidding me. He came home once—once. I could tell by the way he was acting that he couldn't stand to be near me. Who can blame him? HIV is kinda uncool, you know? *(Pause.)* Isn't that all in my file? *(Pause.)* Well, what difference does it make if you read it on a piece of paper or hear it from me? *(Pause.)* Okay, okay! I don't know—I just don't know. I was at the mall with my friends, and this really cute guy was following us all night. We'd go into the Gap, he'd go into the Gap. We went to Waldenbooks, there he was—all night. He finally came up to me in the food court, and well, to make a long story longer, we ended up in his car in the parking lot and three months later I ended up in a clinic getting an abortion. They tested me for HIV at the clinic. *(Pause.)* When? This was about…I don't know, a year ago, maybe. I've known I was positive since they called me.

(Pause.) No. No I never said anything. What was I supposed to say? "Oh, mommy dearest, could you put aside your middle management career and your middle-age crises for a minute? You see, I have this little problem…" What difference would it have made? Would it have stopped me from dying? (Pause.) Oh, please. Spare me your *ABC After School Special* bullshit. I'm gonna die and that's the bottom line. It's all about me, now. For 17 years it's been about my parents, Jason, the dog—anything but me. So, please, all of you—leave me alone. I don't need you or your stupid counseling sessions, 'cause when the lights go out—they're out. Get it?

Lady-Like
Laura Shamas

SARAH PONSONBY: a young woman seeking to escape from an abusive home, 23
SCENE: Ireland, 1778 and Wales

Sarah, an orphan, has been forced to live an unhappy life in the home of her lecherous uncle. When she is finally presented with an opportunity to escape, she confronts her uncle with the intention of blackmailing him for his crimes.

○   ○   ○

SARAH: Uncle. *(She curtsies and starts over.)* I did not wish to see you after the despicable way you've acted for the past months—these actions in the presence of the servants or even Aunt Betty, knowing that she cannot hear. I cannot bear your ugly hands on my breasts or your fingers creeping up my skirt any longer. Further, if you do not give me an allowance so that I may have some freedom, I will make your lecherous actions known…to your daughters, first, so as not to hurt poor Aunt Betty. We'll see how your girls enjoy this information. I'll gather a coterie of other women who have suffered your intentions. Mary, the maid, or Rachel, the cook…Do their names add weight to my request? And finally, in last resort, I will go to Aunt Betty, even though it will hurt her. She would take stock in a woman's lament. These are my terms. Five hundred pounds a year for the rest of my life. And your solemn promise that you will never, never, never touch another woman's body for the rest of your life, or God will strike you dead…Give me money. Thank you, sir. God is watching you to make sure you uphold your end…of the bargain. *(She curtsies.)*

Lady-Like
Laura Shamas

LADY ELEANOR BUTLER: a woman escaping the brutal confines of an unhappy home, 30s
SCENE: Ireland, 1778 and Wales

While in the process of fleeing intolerable lives in Ireland, Eleanor and Sarah travel by boat across the sea to Wales. When Sarah becomes seasick during a gale, Eleanor shares a story from her childhood that she hopes will provide some comfort.

O   O   O

ELEANOR: *(Kneeling beside her.)* When I was little, I'd get seasick on the boat from France to Ireland, when I had to visit home. Of course, I was never ill going from Ireland to France. The nuns, as they would send me off, told me to get to my cabin, lie on the floor with the wood to my back, and to lay my hands beside me, palms down. They told me fairy tales. *(She helps Sarah into that position.)* This way, you are able to feel the pulse of the giant mermen and mermaids who swim underneath the boat, holding it up as they guide it through dangerous waters. They have huge fins that flap with more speed than sails can ever pull. Do you feel them?

[SARAH: Yes…Yes, I feel them.]

ELEANOR: At the end of your journey, you must drop a jewel into the waters to thank them. They are especially fond of emeralds. Green is their color. They're Irish. You must drop a gem into the sea so they will always guide the boats you sail on. Seawings.

[SARAH: Seawings.]

ELEANOR: Seawings to float us all away from troubles. Seawings taking us all from those years of misery, locked away in the castle, rubbing away the pain—

Living in Paradise
Jack Gilhooley

MAX: a college junior trying to emerge from an affluent love-starved adolescence, 20
SCENE: A college dorm room

Max and her mother, a minor film star, have never enjoyed an ideal relationship as may be seen in the young woman's following attempt to communicate via answering machine.

○   ○   ○

MAX: There once was a girl named Maxine
Who left messages on a machine.
Her mother dismissed her,
And Max just got "pissed-er"
Asking, "How could a mom be so mean?"
(Pause.)
Only kidding, Mom. I can't remember the last time we talked, one-on-one. But we will when you return this message. *If* you return it. If I'm not here, please try again.

I'm back at school. Europe was great. Did you get my cards? My phone messages? Where have you been? I wish you'd leave a forwarding address…a phone number on your tape. Yeah, I know. A stranger calling would know where you are…Am I someone you're avoiding?

I'm taking five courses. An elective in screenwriting. Tell Daddy. That might make him happy. Do you two ever talk? Maybe someday he'll give me a job. As a screenwriter. Maybe I'll switch majors. It's not too late. I know he hates theatre. And theatre people. He's not alone, of course. And Film/TV is more practical. Daddy was always the pragmatist…professionally. Today was my first class. The instructor emphasized a "non-cognitive technique"…Objective, impersonal writing. She calls it "dixie cup scripting". Disposable. "Don't take this course to bare your soul," she said. "Forget profundity. Nothing visceral." The most popular writing course on campus and we're learning to write without thought…without feeling. Maybe that's what I need. No one understands my poetry.

How is Marcello? Are you getting married again? Not *again* to him. You haven't married him once.

(Beat.)

Have you? I know you'll tell me if you do. Invite me, perhaps. But that's a ways off. You're not divorced, yet. I never liked Paul but I'm sure he loved you. Probably still does. That counts for something. It counts for a lot. But we're all the caretakers of our own hearts, huh? Or try to be. Easier said than done.

I'm glad you don't have a short telephone tape. Thanks for hearing me out. Please send me a picture. Not another one of those eight-by-ten glossies you send to studios. I'm sorry I tore your picture up last year. It was rage. I'm over that, I think. I've always been envious of your beauty. And to have that gorgeous face…in all those variations…staring at me in a composite…twenty-four hours a day…well, it got to be too much. I apologize.

The photo-bash won't happen again. I've grown a lot, lately. I'd just like a picture of you, relaxed…at ease…natural.

(Smiles.)

Not "au naturel" as in some of your movies. But true to yourself…at a party…playing tennis. The truth is you're sort of a blur to me. Sometimes, when I reflect on you it's through an air-brushed filter. We just don't see enough of one another, Mom. So many of these kids are so happy to be away from their mothers. Not I. I know I gave you a lot of trouble…a lot of grief when I was younger. But I've lurched forward…pinballed my way to a certain maturity. I'm not quite home yet. I should say, "I've not arrived yet." I'm not sure where home is. I'm learning how to get there, though.

My Spanish is excellent now. Three months in Salamanca. Totally immersed in classes. And culture. Now, what do I do with it? I had lots of dates. Nothing serious. I was naive. I thought all that religiosity…those guys would be…reserved…discreet. But they're no longer Catholics. They're hedonists! I guess you could be both. But they're not. Maybe Franco used to put salt-peter in their food. Not anymore. I know you were in Spain with Daddy. When I was small. In one of his movies. I wish you had taken me. But I would not have traveled well. Mothers and daughters dance with each other over there. They walk everywhere, arm-in-arm. At first I thought it was odd. My American sensibility. But then I learned that these women separated by a generation were mother and daughter. Then what had seemed slightly weird…possibly queer…soon became envy.

I went to Granada. I stayed at the parador where you and Daddy had been. I realized that that might have been your last good time together. Next summer, I've got to find a place where you've never been. Then maybe we can go together. You and I. Except that you've been everywhere. Iceland? It's probably nice in the summer. Maybe there's a place you'd like to return to. I wouldn't be a pain in the ass anymore. And I no longer break down. I'm getting through a personal…setback. Right now. It's real. It's deep. But I'm coping. I used to crack over far lesser things. I felt…compelled to call. But not desperate. That was then. If I'm not here when you call back, I'm auditioning. *The Glass Menagerie.* "Laura". A girl with beaucoup problems. But they're not *my* problems. So, I'm removed from the character. And you're not her mother. She traps. You release.

I won't get cast. The director remembers my crazy period. He won't let me play a girl on the edge. But if he'd trust me, I'd surprise him. Surprise you too, Mom.

I had an affair with a man. Not Harry. A man. I thought. I mean, Harry and I had a thing but…

It was a married man. It was *not* meant as an adventure. It was…wish-fulfillment. On my part. Not his. He's still married. He only suggested that it might end. But he suggested it enough to convince me. Once I bought in, he had me. Stupid me.

You warned me about married men. Said it brought you heartache.
(Smile.)

Each and every time. You told me not to commit myself until marriage. Marriage brought you fulfillment…each and every time. You were never the bridesmaid, Mom. Always the bride. Pardon the smart-ass in me but did you give marital advice to Lisa Marie Presley? Take that in the right spirit, huh?

I have no malice toward him. He wants to resume, of course. I don't. Not now. I think I can refrain. Don't ask me his name. You can be vituperative. You'll track him down. Get even for me. But I'm twenty now. I wasn't deceived. Nor did I seduce. It was just…mutual. Love happens. Just like shit. It wasn't a game. Games are fun. What we had was special. But rarely fun. It's my fault. If it's anyone's fault.

And it's over with Harry. He's nice. And cute. But he'll remain a boy as long as he's playing a boy's game. Which should be for a long time. Look him up if he makes "the bigs" and plays in L.A. Sometimes I think he'd be a really interesting guy if his arm went bad. If it all fell apart for him. I don't wish that, though. I just think it would give him dimension. Fast! He's like a lot of kids down here. Bronzed out. Sunstruck. Like in California. It's funny to realize that the last class…

(Pause.)

No, not "funny". It's chilling…to realize that the last class graduated in the Spring. Freshman class, 1990. The last ones to know the killings firsthand. They were different from the rest of us. Apart from age. More quiet. Didn't party as much as the younger classes. But they were especially kind. And sensitive. We'll miss that. Now, it's just a few grad students and the faculty that remembers. We're not so defensive. We don't avoid the buildings where it happened. We're more outgoing. I just spent the day alone—for the most part—with a genuine weirdo. And his ricocheting hormones. Or course, it was Harry's brother but that's hardly reassuring.

Anyway, it's been a full day. A very full day back on campus. I just wanted to talk. And so I have. I'd just like to talk *with* you one of these times.

Hey Mom, a poem. For you. Not a limerick. A real one. Or for me, it's a real one. It's called *Gainesville.*

(She fumbles with a piece of paper and places it close to her light.)

I live in a place of wariness

Young women perfecting peripheral vision

Distaff linkage on the campus of the damned.

Romance, dogma wars, football even, smack of trivia.

Perpetual sunshine…underlying clouds…

We should be immune to terror, the province of others in other lands.

Do others phone home?

We swallow the tension,

Swallow the sweet, sourness of oranges

Aware that life is just a flash

Blocked always am I with you.

Are you with me?

(Slowly she lowers the receiver and the light goes out.)

Love Knots
Vivienne Plumb

LINNEY: the oldest of three sisters mourning the death of their mother, 30-40
SCENE: New Zealand, the present

When their mother dies, the sisters gather at the family home to settle the estate. Here, Linney remembers a summer that was a turning point for their family.

◯   ◯   ◯

LINNEY: *(As if to Blossom.)* Remember that summer Mumma and Dad argued all the time? You had eczema and had to wear little white cotton gloves to stop yourself scratching in the heat. Lou and I lay in our bedroom on our bunk beds and Mumma gave us ice cubes wrapped in a handkerchief to suck. I rubbed them all over myself, over my body, my arms, my face. Dad came home late and Mumma screamed at him. I played outside as much as possible. I'd made a cubby inside a big bush. The branches hung down like a weeping willow and inside the light was green and cool and full of dancing shadows. I was inside my cubby the day I saw Dad with Mrs. Dovey. They were hugging and kissing. I stayed quiet and watched. Their mouths moved like goldfish, then they went off together next door. Months later she came home with Dickie and started to call herself "Missus Dovey". It was around then that Dad left. After Mumma's first heart attack, I told Mrs. Dovey I'd seen her all those years ago with Dad. She told me I should shut up. She said I must have been a regular little spy sitting there under my tree, holding my breath and watching her and Dad through the dancing leaves. They dug up that tree later on. Mumma said the roots had got into the drains. I was glad they dug that one up.

Love Knots
Vivienne Plumb

BLOSSOM: a woman mourning the loss of her mother and her childhood, 20-30
SCENE: New Zealand, the present

Blossom has returned home following a long absence to help her sisters to settle their mother's estate. Blossom and her mother parted on bad terms, and now she finds herself struggling to cope with unresolved feelings of guilt. She makes a project out of digging in the garden for a doll that her mother once buried there and when she finally discovers it, she begins to make a little sense of her memories.

◯   ◯   ◯

BLOSSOM: *(Looking at the doll.)* I always thought this was so beautiful…Everything fades so quickly. All my memories, the pictures in my head of Mumma's face, and even this moment, will fade, crumble away. We never really know what's round the corner. People try to plan and plan their lives, but life shimmers, shifts out of their reach. I can remember when we buried Cha Cha, me squatting here on the edge of the hole we'd dug, my small hand in Mumma's large one while we said a prayer. 'Now we'll bury the angel', she said. She'd won it in the St Vinny's raffle, it was just satin and painted gilt. We buried it with her dead dog Cha Cha. We lay Cha Cha down first, and then the angel on top, and it had looked beautiful then, so holy and full of meaning. *(She lays the angel down.)* Mumma was strong, red-blooded in those days, she could never see herself shrinking, becoming wrinkled and pale. In the end she lost her looks, lost her influence over all of us, became cranky instead of furious. I felt her reaching out to me, trying to hold my youth to her. Her fingers grasped my young smooth wrist as she pressed her lips against my unlined cheek, and I felt the bile rising in me.

Premalal is Buddhist. His white teeth shine at me when he smiles, while he tells me there's another life for us all…Nirvana if we're really good. Don't worry Blossom he says, if you've lived an honest, clean life, and loved your neighbours and animals, you have nothing to fear. But that's just it. I did fear. And I've been so vile. Bitching. Snarking. Ran out on my own little Mumma. And I thought I was digging for the Angel Of Love, but it's dust, just a mirage. *(Laughs a little. Pause.)* It was in the hot Arabian desert that the phoenix burnt itself on a funeral pyre that it had lit with the fanning of its own wings. But of course the next day it rose from the ashes to live over and over again…Once, a long time ago, Mumma told me that story.

Middle-Aged White Guys
Jane Martin

MONA: 40
SCENE: Present, a dump

Mona has decided to leave her husband, Roy, and head west to begin a new life—she tells Roy her thoughts.

☽   ☽   ☽

MONA: I made the journey with you, Roy. I thought I would rest easy and you would care for me. I knew I wasn't a beautiful, wild creature like that R.V., but I thought we could make a quiet life, Roy. That's a horse laugh. A woman's just disposable goods to you. I gave myself over an' forgot who I was, but those days are over and gone, Roy. I'm makin' my own movie now, and you're just something in the rearview mirror to me. I let your tropical fish go free in the creek; I burned your Louis L'Amour first editions, and I pushed your satellite dish off the roof. I'm an outlaw now, Roy, no one will ever treat me that way again.

The Monogamist
Christopher Kyle

SKY: a college student, 21
SCENE: New York City during the Bush administration

Here, a somewhat confused and vaguely nihilistic young woman does her best to explain why she voted for George Bush.

O　　　O　　　O

SKY: So what I'm saying is…What was I saying? Oh, yeah. About the Sixties. The Sixties were obviously this totally cool decade, you know, where everybody was whacked on some major drugs. And you had Morrison, Hendrix, Janis Joplin—all these fucking heroes—Mick Jagger. Okay? And Vietnam, which wasn't cool really, I guess, but it was definitely something to *care* about, which is something about which I don't know *shit.* Caring, I mean, I want to get whacked, sure, but there's no…political content to it, okay? It's just people getting, you know, totally fucked-up and wearing tie-dye shirts. It's a total rip-off of your whole culture and everybody knows it. Okay? Everybody knows it, which is, I guess, why it's cool. It's like totally fake and that's what's…*right* about it. It's like, hey—we don't give a shit about anything, but we're hip to it. Nobody's gonna blow us any shit. Nobody's gonna pull anything on us…like that Watergate, am I right? I bet that caught you by surprise. Not me. I knew what was going down and I was only *four years old.* It's like politics, you know? It's bogus. This whole country's all just…bogus. And that's why I voted for George Bush.
(Pause.)
[DENNIS: Jesus Christ.]
SKY: I mean, the only thing that really *matters,* the only *issue,* is abortion. Okay? I mean, I could march on Washington or some bullshit for that. A woman should be able to choose. Choices—okay?—that's what it's all about. Options. Think about how few choices there used to be at McDonalds. When I was a kid there was, like, hamburger, cheeseburger, fries, shake. That's it. Now it takes half an hour to read the fucking menu. That's options. That's progress.

The Most Massive Woman Wins
Madeleine George

RENNIE: a young woman tortured by her body image, 17
SCENE: A liposuction clinic waiting room

Here, an unhappy young woman details the origins of her yo-yoing weight and the complex emotions that rule her life.

◯   ◯   ◯

RENNIE: The first picture of me is at my first birthday party. In this one I am screaming with laughter and holding my hands up to show the camera that I am covered with chocolate cake. My face is smeared with it, it is all over the front of my pretty pink dress. Apparently I was quite verbally advanced, and my parents were showing me off when my Uncle Jake said, "Oh yeah? How smart is she?" "She's a genius," says my mother, "she understands everything. Try it. She'll do anything you say."

So…"Rennie," says my Uncle Jake, "smush that chocolate cake all over your face, sweetheart. Will you do that for me?"

And I did it of course because I was just that smart and I ruined my dress and they took a picture of me humiliating myself when I was twelve months old. *(Flashbulb pops.)*

This one is my mother's favorite. It's of her and me on one of our mother-daughter days, we're on the steps of the Met looking very close and what you don't see is Mother boring her knuckles into the small of my back saying "Straighten up, sweetheart, it lengthens your neck. Now glow, come on, glow. We want this one to glow."

For awhile there is an absence of photos—when tummies are no longer little-girl cute. Mother hides me at family gatherings and I seem always to end up behind pieces of furniture. So we have no extant record of the long years of wanting, of wanting and wanting and being denied. Reaching for bread and peanut butter and having Slimfast thrust into my twelve-year-old fist. Mother says "No, I am putting my foot down." She is putting her foot down, I see, and I see that to want and demand things is bad.

And when I finally want nothing, nothing at all, when I finally want so little I can barely get up in the morning, my head feels like a ten ton brick on my shoulders, my knees buckle walking from class to class, when I want so little the gentlest sounds scrape my ears and my skin is sore and my hair falls out, finally my mother pulls me out from behind the chaise lounge and says "This is my daughter Rennie! This is my wonderful, beautiful daughter." Out comes the camera!

(Flashbulb pops.)

The pictures reappear. All the while Mother says "Sweetheart, you're beautiful. You really do glow."

(Flashbulb pops.)

In this one I am standing outside my own house, in a hideous dress I do not recall choosing, it is blue and it feels like a garbage bag next to my skin. I am wearing a floppy white orchid on my wrist and man, am I glowing. I am really fucking glowing. My smile is about this wide on my face though I don't know what I am smiling about because Andrew Marino has his hand on my back. We haven't even left the house yet, my mother is still snapping pictures and there he is, slinking his hand up my dress. Later we are in the dark and he is breathing so hard he is fogging the windshield and I say to him Andrew. "No. No." And he says to me "Rennie, you're beautiful. Please Rennie please, will you do it for me?" I am saying, "No," I am saying, Stop, but he does not hear me, I am not loud enough. I am so—weak. I am just...too...weak.

(Flashbulb pops.)

In this one my mother is getting remarried. She is a vision in indigo organdy, she looks half her age, her husband's in real estate. But heavens, where's Rennie? Rennie's not in this one. Rennie is wearing an attractive off-white linen pants suit, but she is not in her place at her mother's side because she is in the parish hall kitchen, devouring the three-foot-tall wedding cake meant to serve one hundred and eighty guests. It was just so pristine, floating there, with no one to guard it, no one to witness...I ate and I ate and I ate it all up until there wasn't one crumb left, not a single frosted rosette, and I held that whole cake inside my body, I had it all to myself. And then I threw it all up on the kitchen floor and I walked out the back door into the night.

My Darling Gremlin
Greg Tate

SEBASTIAN: a New Age mystic, 30s
SCENE: The Nevada/Utah desert near an abandoned nuclear testing site

Sebastian has been reunited with Verdree, an old friend, under the trying circumstances of traveling cross-country on bicycle. Old grievances soon pop up, and before long the two women find themselves arguing over what it means to be black in America. Here, Sebastian points out the difference between their two viewpoints.

SEBASTIAN: *(In a fierce Caribbean accent.)* Woman listen. What being black means to you and what being black means to me are two entirely different things. What it means to you is a bit of yesterday, edging up on today, suddenly staring down an unknown tomorrow. What it means to me encompasses all of eternity and the cosmos. When they say to you, let's talk about being black in America today, *you say* first we must talk about slavery and the Middle Passages. They ask me the same question, I say first we must talk about the distribution ratio of hydrogen and helium atoms in the first moments of the universe's creation. I say, before we talk about being black in America today we must take into consideration how that molecular dispersion accounts for life throughout the known universe. I say before we talk about being black in America today we must go all the way back to the Big Bang. We must discuss black holes, white dwarfs, red giants, superstring theories and invisible dark matter. I say let us first build upon our knowledge of chaos theory and the vibrational affinities that keep nuclear particles from spinning apart. Please stop me if I'm getting too deep for you my sister.

My Virginia
Darci Picoult

JULIE: a woman whose health is compromised by the fact that her mother took the drug DES while she was pregnant, 30s

SCENE: Here and now

When she is released from the hospital following her surgery, Julie withdraws into the world of soap operas until her husband makes an attempt to bring her back to life.

$\bigcirc$　　$\bigcirc$　　$\bigcirc$

JULIE: At least on the soaps,
the plot never changes,
jist who all their sleepin with.
Finally one afternoon, Dan marches into our bedroom
turns off the set and says,
"You and I should have an affair."
"An *Affair?!*" This was too much.
I looked at him and said
"Excuse me honey, did you forget that I am your wife?
Your one and only?…I'm sorry, do I no longer fit the description?…The definition?
Well, lets check it out."
I told him to git me the dictionary.

"I'm not kiddin Dan. Hand over the Webster's. Let's see…Wife…
Definition number one: A Woman.
Definition number two: A Woman actin in a specified capacity.
What capacity Dan? Huh?…I'm not exactly sure what my function is or how I fit in…
To be the mother of your child? Well, check that off the list cause I can't have any. To be your lover? Your mistress? Darlin, I would love to but I…I don't have the time. I am too busy everyday insertin that dilator up my *new* vagina so it don't collapse. I feel like a Goddamn soufflé. A Eunuch. *An It.*
And don't…*Don't* tell me that you understand…
Cause if havin a vagina and bearin children don't separate me from you then I don't know what does.
So I ask you. I beg you. Dan. Please.
Git out of here and leave me alone."

New England
Richard Nelson

ALICE: a woman whose lover has just committed suicide, 54
SCENE: A farmhouse in western Connecticut

When Harry commits suicide, Alice finds herself surrounded by his family, including his twin brother, to whom she reveals Harry's philandering ways.

○   ○   ○

ALICE: About a year ago, Alfred—. *(She ignores Tom.)* Harry started going on and on about this new student of his. A young woman. Said she was—. Amazing. I ran into the two of them one afternoon in the parking lot of the college, chatting. She's beautiful. *(Beat.)* You may see her here tomorrow. I think she's invited herself. *(Beat.)* After seeing her, I said to Harry, what the hell did he take me for? I didn't want any of that. My last husband—. *(She turns to Tom and pats his hand.)* Tom's brother. *(She turns back to Alfred.)* I'd had it with that. I can live alone. I don't mind. *(Beat.)* He smiled—the way he smiled. The way you smile. He was a handsome man. *(Alfred looks up.)* And he kissed me on the lips or tried to. And he said, I don't believe what I'm hearing, Alice. That girl is probably the best violin student I've ever had in America. Her potential is limitless. Finally I feel my talents as a teacher can be fulfilled. You can't know how lucky I feel. Though of course I'm trying to convince her to transfer to Julliard. *(Beat.)* I felt like shit. *(She looks at Tom, then back at Alfred.)* He spent a lot of time with her. He loved teaching. *(Short pause.)* Then one day, I happened by his office door. It was opened a crack. There's also a little window. And there she was with him. She had her violin. I saw her put it under her chin. Raise her bow. And I don't know what I was prepared for, Alfred, but—she was the worst violinist I have ever heard. *(She smiles without looking up.)* I mean it was painful. *(Beat.)* He screwed around all the time. Though after hearing the girl play I realized that there was some suffering on his part as well. It wasn't all... *(Shrugs.)* Maybe even more suffering than pleasure. *(She smiles.)* We can hope.

Our Own Marguerite
Robert Vivian

MARTHA: a young woman struggling to cope with her husband's unexpected disability, 20s
SCENE: Here and now

When Martha's husband, Singer, receives a serious head injury, the quality of their lives rapidly deteriorates. Here, she verbally attacks Singer, who slips in and out of consciousness, and vents all of her frustration and rage.

O   O   O

MARTHA: I'm not about to let this pass, Singer. *(Blows smoke in his face; he coughs.)* You can't fool me. This is my theory: what goes around comes around. I'm not a spiteful woman, but I'll be goddamned if you hoodwink me on this one. I was just 18 when you married me. Remember? Didn't know a thing in the world until *you* taught me. I've learned a few things on my own since. Like how to spot a cheating husband and a bullshitter. Sure I've gained weight. Don't look as pretty as I used to. Is that any reason to go cattin' around behind my back *for ten years?* *(Beat.)* I worshipped you, Singer; you swept me off my feet and I thought you were the gentlest, kindest man ever. You never told me you were married before. That you had some kid running around with your ears and face and shock of black hair. I had to discover that on my own. How is that supposed to feel? That I wasn't the only one and never would be when all along you were my first and only? Would you have kids with me? Hell, no, wouldn't dream of it. Now you're a mannequin. A melon with hair. *(Beat.)* I hate your guts, Singer. Look what you've done to us, living on that measely disability check and my housecleaning. What a life. What a fucking life. And everything was so bright once, when you were straight with me and…devoted. Or was that a lie, too? *(Beat.)* You did this to us…Way before your accident. And when I broke down you said, Get your shit together. *Me! Get my shit together! When all along it was me that made this stinking pit a home!* *(Beat.)* It just took me forever to realize I was the only one in it. Until that crane hit you in the head. Then everything changed and you're all sorry now, all quiet and respectful. Bullshit. It don't wash—not with me anymore. *(Holds up statue.)* And Betty gave us this because she couldn't believe how sloppy we lived, what pigs we are. I saw it in her eyes. I used to care. But not anymore. *(Holds statue close to his face.)* So go on; worship her. It's no different than before.

The Psychic Life of Savages
Amy Freed

ANNE BITTENHAND: a poet, 40s
SCENE: Here and now

Following a doomed affair with the American Poet Laureate, Anne has decided to take the final plunge. Here, she prepares to take her own life.

○   ○   ○

ANNE: Most gals would dress in their best black for the most important date of their lives. Not me. For you, honey, I'm putting on the softest blue dress with a mauve scarf. I've always known that you like the most tender colors. *(She begins to dress and make up her face.)*
Just make yourself comfortable. I won't be long. The thing I like about you is, I don't have to maintain any mystery. We've been intimate for years. I've always thought you were a real softy. The one that loved a girl for what she was inside. You really want to get inside. Not just inside the way most guys want to, but you want to tear a girl apart the way other men only dream of. And I'll tell you what. I don't think it will be so bad. I think it will be all right. When I first saw lines around my eyes and mouth, when my knees first started to get a little baggy, my trim brown knees, I cried. I thought you were the enemy, the corroding tide that would carry me farther and farther away from the shores of love. Men all say I'll love you when you're old, but they only like to say it to you when you're really young. They can't do it, poor things, they'd like to but they just can't. But you. You've been gentle, you've been slow. But you've rained your constant acid kisses down on my poor flesh since the day I first bloomed. And you've never left my side. It's been you, perched jealously at the top of every bed where I groaned in joy. It's been you sucking away my beauty through a twenty-year-long straw. And now I understand that it's because you love me. You love me so truly you've been sucking me out of myself. Blasting my body so that I'll leave it finally, to be with you. You want to eat me. Well, I surrender. I don't know what it will be like. But I think maybe you know more about this than I.

The Psychic Life of Savages
Amy Freed

ANNE BITTENHAND: a poet, 40s
SCENE: Here and now

Anne is a dangerously self-absorbed woman who uses her poetry as an outlet for her psychoses. She has recently signed herself into a mental institution following an unpleasant scene at her daughter's birthday party and here complains to her husband, Tito, on the phone.

$\qquad$ O $\qquad$ O $\qquad$ O

(A Mental Institution. Anne is on phone. Rebecca, a young mental patient, is sitting on the floor drawing on a large pad.)

ANNE: I'm OK, I'm not OK I'm OK. Stop yelling at me! Would I be back in the nuthouse again if I knew why I did it! Use your head, Tito! I'm sorry lover. I can't really make sense of it to you. Because you won't—no, you don't—do you remember that thing I was describing? What happened last week at the hairdresser's, where the tops of the trees started forming into a hostile pattern? I can just tell! For God's sake!

(Pause.)

Don't you think I'd rather be home taking the lamb chops out of the oven? Or whatever you cook them in. If I could cook, I mean. Its not a matter of making an effort! I have a time bomb in my brain, and it just, *Went Off!* That's all.

(Pause.)

Did my agent call? Well, why didn't you say so? They're taking *Thoughts On My First Bleeding Time!* That's wonderful! Did you tell her where I was?

(Pause.)

Listen! My readers do not *care* that I'm a *nut!* My readers *love* that I'm a nut. So tell her. No, Baby, not this weekend!

Because, I can't handle it, that's why. Don't you understand that it's a little hard for me to be playing wife and mother for you and our daughter right now? I just feel like the whole world is one big stinking gas chamber! Don't come up yet!

The Queen's Knight
Frank Cossa

MARIE-ANTOINETTE: former Queen of France
SCENE: Paris, October 1793

On the evening before she is to appear before the Revolutionary Tribunal, Marie-Antoinette is visited in her prison cell by Chauveneau-Lagarde, the idealistic young attorney who has been commanded to defend her. When he asks that she beg the Tribunal for a postponement, she flatly refuses and offers the following explanation.

    O   O   O

QUEEN: I have been a prisoner of these people for four years. I watched them march to the gates of the palace and slaughter six hundred Swiss guards. I watched as all my friends were murdered or driven into exile. I watched them execute my husband who was their King. I watched them drag my children screaming from my arms so that after a year I don't know if they're alive or dead. I have lived in this room for seventy-six days. They allow me two dresses, no undergarments, no cloak, no blanket against the dampness that runs down the walls. There is never any fire wood. There is always a guard outside my cell who must keep his eyes on me at all times. *At all times.* Some days ago the Princess de Lamballe, my last loyal friend, returned from a safe exile to be near me in my difficult time. She came here to visit me. The mob saw her and I watched them tear her to pieces. Her head was impaled on a stake and raised up to my window there.
(She points.)
One man made himself moustaches out of her private hair while the others, laughing and cheering, threw parts of her...her body up at me. You see, monsieur, for four years one horror has followed another. They have allowed me no comfort, no rest. They have spared me no cruelty, no shock, no terror. And you wish me to ask these people for...
(She turns, slowly again, to look at him.)
a *favor?*

The Queen's Knight
Frank Cossa

MARIE-ANTOINETTE: former Queen of France
SCENE: Paris, October 1793

When the former Queen is questioned by her attorney on the evening before she is to appear before the Tribunal, their dialogue eventually devolves into a philosophical discussion of human rights. When her attorney insists that people are born with such rights, Marie-Antoinette is quick to correct such a notion.

○　　　○　　　○

QUEEN: I think not. I think they acquired them very suddenly. I had never heard such words in my life before and then suddenly I heard nothing else. You chided me earlier for acting according to fashion, but I think all that has happened to me has been nothing more than changing fashions. Before I was born my country made an alliance with France, against all history and tradition, because there was a *fashion* for all things French. I was chosen to seal the bargain because I was the prettiest and the stupidest of my mother's daughters—exactly what the French would want. I was educated to dance and smile, as was *fashionable*. Did you know that when I came here I could barely write a coherent sentence? Only by then it had become *fashionable* to be intelligent, witty, to quote Montesquieu, Voltaire, Diderot. I, of course, had never heard of any of those gentlemen. Suddenly it was fashionable to mock, to mock everything, the King, the Pope, God even! To be cynical, to be flippant, to believe in nothing. Then came the Americans with their charming, rustic manners, the squinting lecher Franklin, the sweet intellectual Jefferson, with their droll stories and perpetual need for French money. So our money and our young noblemen went to America. The money never came back. The young men did, full of stories of their romantic sojourn abroad. They brought with them democracy and the pox in equal measure. We survived the pox.

Saucy Jack
Sharon Pollock

KATE: a music hall entertainer, 35
SCENE: Chiswick, England, December 1, 1888

Kate has been hired by James Kenneth Stephen, scholar and one-time tutor of Prince Albert Victor, heir to the throne of England. On a December evening, James pays Kate to reenact the brutal deaths suffered by the prostitutes slaughtered by the killer know as Jack the Ripper for the benefit of the Prince, who is implicated in the crimes. Here, Kate confronts the Prince with the most gruesome death of Catherine Eddowes.

○　　　○　　　○

KATE: I'm in love! I'm in love and love's got no perimeters!
(Eddy looks to Jem for assistance and guidance, disconcerted by Kate's retaining his cloak, them moves back into the room. Kate stalks him.)
It's bigger than London and stretches further than Kent! That's a long stretch when you're hoofin' it to pick hops and the weather turns bad and back the two a you come with nothing' in your pocket but a coupla pence and a pawn ticket for a shirt! And me love's name's John and we pawned his boots and I said you go to the doss house 'cause he's not well and I'll stay on the street. He's a fine featured man and he's got bright eyes and his last name's Kelly. And I love him, oh I do, and he loves me.
(She confronts Eddy.)
Yes, love!
Looove!
(She includes Jem in her confrontation.)
Love love love love love!!
And when he saw my lyin' in the Golden Lane Mortu'ry there—
(She throws Eddy's cloak to the floor centre stage.)
disemboweled like a pig, with me eyelids nicked—
(She moves after Eddy in a more threatening way than previously.)
and me poor nose cut off and the skin a me cheeks flayed and a lobe a me ear caught in the folds a me skirt, he wept, he cried out, and he went round to the constables there and he was worse for drink and—
(She rushes at Eddy.)

he knocked them down and he yelled out loud "If I was you and charged with walking the Whitechapel beat—

(Eddy has sought safety behind Jem's chair, Kate faces Jem in the chair and Eddy behind it.)

"If I was the copper in Mitre Square when he struck her down and ripped her up! I'd've killed myself!! I'd've killed myself!!

(Jem stands up, Kate backs down in a way.)

"I'd kill myself!!"

(She retreats up stage. Pause as Jem and Eddy watch her. She draws herself up and continues.)

His name's John Kelly! He's a good man. We had seven years together. And there was never a time that I went on the street but it pained him and it hurt him!

(Jem begins to advance on her but she stands her ground.)

But we had a desperate need for money!

For a bit a tea! Or a—or a piece of bread!

Or a doss bed when the weather was bad and he wasn't well, and a single doss is four pence you know and it takes you two to get you that!! It doesn't seem right. He worked hard. Porter he was but there's not always work, and sometimes so weak he couldn't finish the end of a day. But I loved him.

(Jem is getting closer to her.)

It was somethin' special. And he loved me. I could see it in his eyes. Bright they were. And I could hear his cry when he looked down, down at me face and he knew it was me. Catherine Eddowes! Sometimes Kate! Sometimes Jane! Sometimes Mary Ann! Sometimes Kelly! Catherine Eddowes, born Wolverhampton 1842; died Mitre Square, Sunday, September 30, 1888.

(She runs, grabs the knife left on the side board by Eddy, and turns on Jem pointing the knife at him aggressively. She sings.)

Praise God from whom all blessings flow!

Self-Defense
Michael P. Scasserra

WOMAN: recently discovered her birth mother, 20-30
SCENE: Here and now

Here, a woman details her search for her biological parents and goes on to explain how it has affected her eating habits.

O   O   O

(A woman, about thirty, enters. She has a slightly preppie appearance and carries a large purse. She takes a bag of food out of the purse. During her monologue, she takes out small individually wrapped food items which she sets in a row before her: a slice of apple, a carrot stick, a small bottle of water, and a candy bar.)

WOMAN: I always wanted to find out who my real mother was
not because I was emotionally needy
but just because I was curious.
Growing up an adopted child,
my fantasy was that my parents were
Florence Henderson and Robert Reed.
Then, when I was in high school,
Joni Mitchell and Neil Young.

So, what do I come to find out?
My birth mother was actually an overweight neurotic from Queens
who was supposedly the victim of a rape
committed by an Iraqi exchange student.
I ask you,
do I look Iraqi?
I find the woman's story hard to believe.

Now because I had so many years
to think about what my real mother would be like
it was kind of anticlimatic when I got the phone call
only nine days after I put the application in to A.L.M.A.
A.L.M.A.
Adoptees Liberty Movement Association.

They told me
A. I was the product of a rape
at which point I thought
"Holy shit,
do I really want to hear this?"
But, of course, I did
and A.L.M.A. went on to say that
B. My birth mother has been dead since 1989
but that
C. She had been actively looking for me since 1980
which struck me as disgusting
because she apparently waited until I was eighteen
so she'd have no financial obligation to me.

But in her defense,
her dead defense,
I found out that she had a very sad life.

The high point of her search for me was an impassioned appearance
on *Geraldo*.
I was moved, of course, that she was looking for me
but going on *Geraldo*.
Sensationalism run amok!

I got a videotape of the show and watched it
expecting to discover some missing piece of myself
but when I saw my mother,
I thought I would cry.
Imagine the horror of finding someone who looks exactly like you
but is about two hundred pounds overweight.
Your features
but on a face like a balloon.
I looked at her,
then at myself.
It was like looking at the before and after in a Slim-Fast ad.
I never felt so pretty and so thin in my life.
But I'm playing it safe.
I'm now into macrobiotics,

fighting what I fear is my biological fate.
It's not only what you eat,
but the order in which you eat it.
(She finishes putting out the row of food, studies it.)
Something's not right.
(She pulls a large diet book from her purse and goes to a marked page,
reads, then switches the order of carrot and the bottle of water.)
That's it.
You see, the proper order, if I can eat these three,
I can eat the chocolate last,
and then it will all be flushed out of my system
rather than ferment in my digestive tract
thus causing obesity.
(She starts eating the apple.)
I really resent having to do this.
Because of this woman's lack of self-control,
I have eaten enough beans and rice
to give all of Rhode Island the runs.

Anyway, I did go to meet the rest of "the family"
and all I could think when I met them was,
"Thank god."
Thank god these people gave me up!
If they'd kept me,
I'd be working behind the lingerie counter at Sear's by now.

They live in Queens,
the last nice neighborhood in Queens,
they told me on the phone.
So I went,
with great fear and trepidation,
to meet "the family" in Queens.
I had on this new outfit from Barney's,
purchased just with the intention of meeting these people.
Well, I blew them all away,
looks-wise, brains-wise, taste-wise, everything-wise.
Turns out this family is white trash.
But they have plenty of money.

Financially secure white trash.
I mean that in the nicest possible way.
I get there,
there are all these fat women with big hair
and they're coming at me with combs to tease me all up
and I said
"No hands, no touching."
I meet my half-sister
also fat
who, it turns out
tells me that she makes all of her own clothes.
She *makes* them.
They had an adorable impromptu buffet for me,
a table full of fats, sugars, and red meats.
Oh,
and I meet my mother's father
who keeps insisting that I call him "Grampy,"
could you die?
So "Grampy" decided that he wants to buy me a savings bond
and he asked me for my social security number.
Frankly, I found his request intrusive.
I mean, how dare he?
I could see a trust fund perhaps,
but a savings bond?
I don't want to feel obligated to these people in any way.
I feel no bond at all.
I now have a greater appreciation for my adoptive family,
who I love very much,
and I'm very secure in my own identity
so I can't be influenced by all this biology shit.
Although the weight thing has got me in a tizzy.
But by this time in my life
I'm a bitch
I'm a snot
and it's gloriously deep-rooted.

The whole experience has been like a nightmare.

So now, I'm looking for my father
who may or may not be
an aging Iraqi rapist with a 1965 degree from Rutgers.
God only knows what I will find.
(She finally has worked her way to the candy bar.)
Finally.
(Unwraps the candy bar and indulges in a bite.)

Sophistry
Jonathan Marc Sherman

ROBIN: a young woman delivering the valedictory speech at her commencement, 20
SCENE: A New England college campus, 1990

Robin here does her best to make sense of her four years as an undergraduate.

○   ○   ○

ROBIN: When I was a little girl, I was so *confident* and *certain,* daydreaming in my suburban Illinois bedroom, all nice and safe and clean and frilly. My parents, who are here right now—wave to the crowd, folks. *(Points.)* That's them. They used to make me settle fights with my playmates. They'd call them *debates,* but don't let that fool you. They were fights. *(Beat.)* This school's administrators recently paid an enormous sum of money to *settle.* To keep a former professor from taking them to court to challenge a decision *they* made. This doesn't feel like a fight, or a debate—not really. This feels like compromise. This feels...very *Hollow.* What is this supposed to mean to us, as we're about to graduate from this place, with diplomas from an institution that's telling us to settle? *(Beat.)* I know that eventually, when understanding runs out, there is a need for judgment, but *who* is qualified to judge? And who is qualified to *judge* who is qualified to judge? Who picks the judges? Who decides that it's okay—to settle? *(Beat.)* Everybody in my hometown was shocked when I chose this place, but they shouldn't have been. Martha Graham danced here. I used to envision myself—secretly, of course—as the heir apparent to Martha Graham. Here was a *woman* making exotic *shapes*—her shapes made more powerful statements than all the tainted rhetoric in the air. *(Beat.)* If I could only *dance* all of this...*(Pause.)* But...I can't. *(Beat.)* I've tried to find some truth during my time here, some *wisdom,* beyond food and sleep and sex and *showers.* What's worth giving to? I don't know. I wish I did. *(Beat.)* I suppose *settling* can also mean coming to some sort of peace, and I do hope we all find some sort of peace in our lives...*All* of us. Anybody...anybody who's ever been in pain. And whether *we* settle or...*not*...remains to be seen.

Talk/Show
Michael P. Scasserra

WOMAN: describing her upcoming cosmetic surgery, 40-50
SCENE: Here and now

Here, a woman shares her plans for a facelift with a television audience.

○   ○   ○

WOMAN: Oh my.
Oh, my goodness.

You'll excuse me,
but I've never been on television before
and I'm more than a little disturbed
by seeing myself on the monitor.
It's sort of a shock.

But…
focus.

I have been instructed to remember
that my mission here is to be open and frank
but to watch the use of "questionable language."
My ex-husband was a linguist at N.Y.U.
and he used to say
"All language is questionable."
He was such a bore.

But, who cares about him.
He is in the past.
I am in the present.

I am here
in order to talk about my very important plans
plans some of my friends and family members believe
I should be less willing to discuss in public

due to the highly sensitive, personal nature of these plans…
but I don't feel that way.

We need to share
we of today's difficult cold world
in which so very many speak
yet so few listen.

You see
it has taken me a long time
and a great deal of quite expensive professional consultation
to reach the conclusions I have reached
and if I can save even one person out there
some part of the grueling search through
which I have been…
well, that would be enough…
to touch one other human being.

Focus.
I must often remind myself to focus…
and to be accurate…
my ex-husband told me that I was inaccurate…
"inaccurate but consistent," he would say…
I never understood that…
he had a low sperm count.

Anyway.
My plans.

(Stands up to demonstrate for the camera.)
Can you get this all on?

Exactly one week from tomorrow
an overpriced but brilliant surgeon
will take a small steel blade
and make two minute incisions just below my eyelids.
From there, he will remove excess tissue and tighten the skin.
At a later date
fat and excess skin will be removed
from my buttocks and outer thighs

and my abdomen will be tightened.
I will be having a mastopexy…
that's a breast lift…
as well as equalization of breast size.
My new nose
the one my inner-being has always had,
will look natural and
blend smoothly
he assures me
with the face-lift
the incisions for which will fade in a few months
into my hairline and around the edges of my ears.

I had wanted to do something
about the lines developing across my forehead
but my doctor informed me that this can only be done
by a process which destroys muscles in the forehead
and that this reduces or eliminates facial expression
as well as the ability to lift one's eyebrows.
So
he explained to me
that I would never be able to express surprise again.
I thought about this and
although I decided that the older one gets
the less there is to be surprised about
I decided to forgo that procedure for the time being.

So…
after all this working of miracles
I will be left as youthful as a drum
and as tight as a teenage girl.
No!
I reversed it…
sorry…
as tight as a drum
and as youthful as a teenage girl.

Tough Choices For the New Century
Jane Anderson

ARDEN SHINGLES: 30s
SCENE: Southern California, present

Arden teaches workshops and seminars on self-defense. Here she "works" a crowd.

$\bigcirc$ $\bigcirc$ $\bigcirc$

ARDEN: Take a look at this chart. This is the reality, folks. I wish I could say that things in our country were getting better but sweet people, all you have to do is look at the numbers. And with all the riots, floods, fires, earthquakes, droughts—with all this happening, more and more people are saying, "Hey, the world's coming to an end, I don't give a blankety-blank about the law." You know? And the rest of us, the good people, the ones who, as Bob said, practice preparedness—we're going to have our little supply boxes with our batteries and canned goods, whatever, that we so carefully put together, and what's going to stop someone from walking up to us and saying, "Gimme"? And I hear, "Oh, I know it's really bad out there but there's nothin' I can do about it. Boo-hoo," you know? And I meet so many people, especially women who support this nondefense kind of attitude. They say, "Oh, I don't want to have a gun, my boyfriend says it's not feminine." Well what's feminine? *(Pause.)* You know? What's feminine—to look at me, I think you'd say that I was "feminine." Bob, would you say I was feminine?

Twelve Dreams
James Lapine

DOROTHY TROWBRIDGE: an unhappy woman undergoing psychotherapy, 30s
SCENE: A New England College town, 1936

Wealthy and disturbed, Dorothy seeks deliverance from the demons of her past in the care of Dr. Hatrick, a psychiatrist. After months of fruitless sessions, Dorothy finally reveals the source of her pain.

◯   ◯   ◯

TROWBRIDGE: *(She speaks, her voice slowly becomes that of a child.)* He was the most beautiful man I have ever seen. Dark. Tall. I wasn't a pretty girl. I was awkward. They never let me dress my age. I was kept a child. Boys never paid attention to me. I never even understood such matters.

William. William came to the house one day—to bring something from the factory. I had just come out of the bath. I was wearing a cotton robe—nothing else. My hair was down. I heard the car and went to the window. There he was. I just stared at him from the window. He later told me the sunlight flooded in so—in through my gown—that he could see me beneath the cotton. We smiled at one another, then he drove off.

[HATRICK: Then what?]

TROWBRIDGE: That night, I happened to look out my window, and I saw him sitting across the street. Night after night, the same. Finally, one evening, Mama and Papa were at the theatre. The servants were in their quarters, and I snuck out.

[HATRICK: And what happened?]

TROWBRIDGE: It just seemed so normal. He made me feel so wonderful. I had never been happier.

[HATRICK: Go on.]

TROWBRIDGE: It continued—whenever I could escape. I loved him. Then my body began to change. I was so stupid. I didn't even understand. I thought it was a part of nature—growing up. It was nature all right. Sickness in the morning. Mama heard me ill one day and insisted that I see a doctor.

[HATRICK: Please finish the story.]

TROWBRIDGE: *(Back into adult voice; bitter.)* Mama fell to pieces. She couldn't cope. Papa became a crazed man. I was forbidden to leave the house. At night, I would look out my window but William was never there—Father saw to that. My world just stopped. I never had the chance to explain. To at least say good-bye. I never saw him again. I knew I wouldn't.

[HATRICK: What of the child?]

TROWBRIDGE: Elaborate plans were made to send me abroad. The deception was carried to great lengths. All I could think of was seeing him. There was a terrible row—Mama, Papa and me, all screaming at each other in the library. I completely lost control. Unraveled with feelings of hate. God, I hated them! I hated myself even more.

(Cold, distant.)

I guess I thought if I could change my circumstances, I could go back; go back to how it was. I ran to my room and locked myself in and with my fist— I began to beat myself. I felt no pain as I pounded my stomach with all the force I could—I beat myself until...how could they have done that...how could I have done that to my...

Watbanaland
Doug Wright

FLO: a woman desperate to have a baby, 30s
SCENE: Here and now

Flo's husband has refused to have sex with her for over a year. The worst part is that he seems incapable of offering an explanation for his unexpected aversion. Here, Flo offers a glimpse of ·.her inner torment.

○　　　○　　　○

FLO: I have a pupil. Ruthie. She has the smell of talcum, and her skin boasts a rosiness I've seen in nineteenth century portraiture more often than in life. Playing near the swing-set, when the sun strikes her, she surpasses Cassatt. Today I watched her play for the better part of an hour. She took a doll from its wooden bed. She sat with it till the morning's end, rocking and singing softly. Her fluid eyes stared with wonder into it's painted ones. When it was time to nap, she cradled it next to her breast as she slept.

Her own mother came to retrieve her at the end of the day. Ruthie saw her and broke into unabashed squeals. Her mother laughed too, and knelt down. Ruthie ran to her. They folded into one another. Her mother stood, Ruthie's legs wrapped around her torso. The child seemed to extend, full-blown, from her mother's belly.

Ruthie still held the doll, like a torch. Its arms twisted in exultation and its head faced backwards. It sprouted forth, like an extra limb, from Ruthie's grasp. The children, real and imagined, were glorious branches, splitting off and reaching toward the sky, taking flight from their parent tree.

I watched the three of them and I wished—with all my heart—for an ax to chop them down.

(Flo shifts her gaze, regarding Park in the mirror.)

Deliver me. Deliver me from that.

Your Obituary Is A Dance
Benard Cummings

NELLA RAE: 30s, heavyset

Nella tells how she overcame her poor self-concept as a black woman.

○   ○

NELLA: But, baby, when the Truth finally shined its light down on me, and I saw just how *sweet* my blackness was—*sweet,* do you hear me now?…

[TOMMY: …I hear you…]

NELLA: …I got all those tired asses up off this pussy. When Otis finally came into my life all them years ago…you remember…

[TOMMY: …sho' do…]

NELLA: …and told me, "Man can't live on your pussy alone, but by every word of love that proceedeth out of your mouth", I thought that he was crazy as hell. But he *loved* me, baby. And I'm still with his big ol' rusty ass 'cause he showed me 'the darker the night, the brighter the day.' See…my people, my people…folks used to make fun of my berry-black blackness when I was growing up. And now you can't seem to turn around without Black folks acting like the last dark African on God's green earth. Folks wearing more Kente cloth and beads and shit than anybody from Africa wears. All of a sudden it's politically fashionable to be what they tortured me about as a child. And all of it because folks *now* talkin' 'bout some "Afro-American" identity and "reclaiming our roots" and whatnot. Makes me want to scream "Hell, everybody knows we from Africa 'cept us!" I'll just be damned…